This Book Belongs To

Christmas

Content by **Gooseberry Patch Company**
Artwork by **Gooseberry Patch Company**

LEISURE ARTS
Vice President and Editor-in-Chief: Anne Van Wagner Childs
Executive Director: Sandra Graham Case
Administrative Coordinator: Debra Nettles
Design Director: Patricia Wallenfang Sowers
Test Kitchen Director/Foods Editor: Celia Fahr Harkey, R.D.
Editorial Director: Susan Frantz Wiles
Publications Director: Kristine Anderson Mertes
Creative Art Director: Gloria Bearden
Licensed Product Coordinator: Lisa Truxton Curton

EDITORIAL STAFF

EDITORIAL
Managing Editor: Linda L. Trimble
Associate Editor: Janice Teipen Wojcik
Assistant Editor: Marjorie Ann Lacy
Copy Editor: Terri Leming Davidson

TECHNICAL
Senior Technical Writer: Marley N. Washum
Technical Writers: Sherry Solida Ford, Jennifer S. Hutchings,
   Susan McManus Johnson, Laura Lee Powell,
   Barbara McClintock Vechik and Theresa Hicks Young
Technical Assistant: Linda Luder
Copy Editor: Susan Frazier
Production Assistant: Sharon Gillam

FOODS
Assistant Foods Editor: Jane Kenner Prather
Foods Copy Editor: Judy Millard
Test Kitchen Home Economist: Rose Glass Klein
Test Kitchen Coordinator: Nora Faye Taylor
Test Kitchen Assistants: Brandy Black Alewine,
   Camille T. Alstadt and Donna Huffner Spencer

DESIGN
Designers: Polly Tullis Browning, Diana Sanders Cates,
   Cherece Athy Cooper, Cyndi Hansen, Dani Martin,
   Sandra Spotts Ritchie, Billie Steward, Anne Pulliam Stocks
   and Linda Diehl Tiano
Executive Assistant: Debra Smith

ART
Book/Magazine Graphics Art Director: Diane M. Thomas
Senior Graphics Artist: Linda Lovette Smart
Graphics Artist: Faith R. Lloyd
Photography Stylists: Beth Carter, Ellen J. Clifton, Karen Hall,
   Aurora Huston and Christina Myers
Publishing Systems Administrator: Cynthia M. Lumpkin
Publishing Systems Assistant: Myra S. Means

PROMOTIONS
Managing Editor: Alan Caudle
Associate Editor: Steven M. Cooper
Designer and Graphics Artist: Dale Rowett

BUSINESS STAFF
Publisher: Rick Barton
Vice President and General Manager: Thomas L. Carlisle
Vice President, Finance: Tom Siebenmorgen
Vice President, Retail Marketing: Bob Humphrey
Vice President, National Accounts: Pam Stebbins
Retail Marketing Director: Margaret Sweetin
General Merchandise Manager: Cathy Laird
Distribution Director: Rob Thieme
Retail Customer Service Manager: Wanda Price
Print Production Manager: Fred F. Pruss

Library of Congress Catalog Number 99-71586
Hardcover ISBN 1-57486-151-4
Softcover ISBN 1-57486-167-0

10 9 8

Gooseberry Patch Co.

Christmas

Merry ideas, recipes & how-to's for the happiest of holidays!

A LEISURE ARTS PUBLICATION

Christmas

Gooseberry Patch

Family & Friends are delighted to share with you our yummy recipes, whimsical artwork & holiday crafts.

How Did Gooseberry Patch Get Started?

You may know the story of Gooseberry Patch...the tale of two country friends who decided one day over the backyard fence to try their hands at the mail order business. Started in JoAnn's kitchen back in 1984, Vickie & JoAnn's dream of a "Country Store in Your Mailbox" has grown and grown to a 96-page catalog with over 400 products, including cookie cutters, Santas, snowmen, gift baskets, angels and our very own line of cookbooks! What an adventure for two country friends!

Through our catalogs and books, Gooseberry Patch has met country friends from all over the world. While sharing letters and phone calls, we found that our friends love to cook, decorate, garden and craft. We've created Kate, Holly & Mary Elizabeth to represent these devoted friends who live and love the country lifestyle the way we do. They're just like you & me... they're our "Country Friends®!"

Your friends at Gooseberry Patch

Mary Elizabeth   Holly   Kate   Spotty

Contents

Make it merry, Wrap it bright

Gifts From the Kitchen

Festive Foods & Glorious Feasts

FAMILY CHRISTMAS CHERISHED TRADITIONS

Along with mistletoe and holly, the Christmas season brings warm thoughts of holidays spent with loved ones. Refresh these memories with photos of Christmases past displayed in charming albums and frames. Set out nostalgic mementos like antique books and children's blocks in eye-catching arrangements. Start a collection of snowmen, Santas or angels...or start a family tradition like taking a Christmas hayride or hosting a Christmas card-addressing party. Have a ball this Christmas...and remember that the special ways you choose to celebrate the holidays now will become the traditions you honor in years to come.

Keep the magic of Christmas close at hand with our family traditions photo album. Instructions for this treasure keeper are on page 120.

To make a tree skirt to treasure...lightly brush your children's hands with water-soluble paint and have them gently press their handprints onto a length of unbleached muslin.

Make an album for your children. Feature all the wonderful things they've done the past year!

Let your child design your holiday cards this year! Take a favorite piece of his or her "refrigerator art" to your local copy shop. Ask them to reduce the artwork to fit onto a folded sheet of paper, then copy the artwork onto a nice, heavy stock. Purchase envelopes to fit and send out as cards. Won't Grandma and Grandpa be proud!

Or turn your child's drawings into Christmas notepads!

Surprise a friend or a grandparent with a small child's voice on their telephone answering machine. When you know for sure they aren't home, telephone them and have your child sing "Twinkle, Twinkle, Little Star," "Jingle Bells" or "Away in a Manger." These little songs should be enough to make anyone's day delightful.

Trace your children's hands on a plain tablecloth. Add their names and ages and the year, too!

A happy childhood is one of the best gifts that parents have in their power to bestow. – R. CHOLMONDELEY

Capture the special moments of your life by creating keepsake treasures! Instructions for baby's first ornament and our appliquéd frame are on pages 120-121.

Pictures bring back the fondest memories. Don't forget to take photographs of the everyday joys of the holidays...Dad stringing the outside lights, the kids rolling out cookie dough, Mom wrapping presents, cozy pictures of the family just curling up by the fire. And keep the camera handy during the holidays to snap pictures of kids with cookie faces, rosy cheeks and happy smiles!

Keep a "Holiday Memories" photo book of all your Christmas parties and dinners. Children and grandchildren will love to page through all the memories of good times shared...a wonderful legacy to pass on.

Far-away family members love to see updated pictures of your family. Round everyone up around the tree, including family pets, dress in festive sweaters, put the kids in holiday striped pajamas...have fun! If you take this Christmas photograph of your family in the same place, same position each year, you'll have a record of how the kids have grown.

Videotape family members and loved ones during the holidays...telling stories, singing songs, recalling the "olden" days! These are our best Christmas keepsakes.

"I ALWAYS TAKE A CHRISTMAS EVE PHOTO OF MY KIDS IN THEIR JAMMIES IN FRONT OF THE TREE."

"I WRITE A LETTER TO SANTA EVERY YEAR — AND I HAVE EVERY YEAR SINCE I CAN REMEMBER. MY MOM KEPT ALL MY LETTERS (AFTER FORWARDING A COPY TO SANTA, OF COURSE) AND IT'S A TRADITION TO RE-READ THEM EVERY CHRISTMAS EVE. WHAT FUN TO SEE WHAT A 9-YEAR-OLD-ME WANTED!"

Make a grouping of well-loved toys and stuffed animals surrounded with greenery and ribbons.

Bring your favorite childhood Teddy bear down from the attic. Place him under the Christmas tree...sure to rekindle fond memories!

Create a tree just for your children...use fun themes such as a doll's tea party or their favorite sport! Secure special toys or stuffed animals with wire to the Christmas tree for a toy theme that will bring smiles and memories to your visitors!

Pile children's toys in a decorated bushel basket! Paint the basket a country color inside and out. When dry, hand-letter their names on the front!

Dress up a keeping room or kitchen cupboard with children's toys, ornaments, wreaths and votive candles. Use favorite collectibles and greeting cards too!

Help your daughter decorate her doll's house for Christmas with tiny wreaths and ornaments.

Use old-fashioned bubble lights and greenery as a centerpiece to conjure up childhood memories.

Have Santa leave a special treat for the kids. On Christmas Eve, hang a wreath of greens on your child's bedroom door. Decorate the wreath with tiny treasures...old tops, small Teddy bears, pretty pink ballet slippers...what a wonderful way for your child to greet Christmas day!

Since Christmas brings out the child in all of us, it's natural to celebrate the holidays by recalling childhood memories. Blend the nostalgia of youth with Christmas tradition by spelling out season's greetings with old-fashioned building blocks; add your favorite holiday accents.

OUR ALL ★ TIME FAVORITE CHRISTMAS BOOKS

MARY ELIZABETH:
THE SNOWMAN by RAYMOND BRIGGS

HOLLY:
NIGHT BEFORE CHRISTMAS by CLEMENT C. MOORE

KATE:
THE POLAR EXPRESS by CHRIS VAN ALLSBURG

SPOTTY:
CARL'S CHRISTMAS by ALEXANDRA DAY

Start a collection of Christmas books! Look for them at garage sales and secondhand book shops. Display the books in a basket by a cozy chair. Let your children choose one to read before bedtime each night during the holidays, or set aside a night to gather family around and read all your favorites together.

There's a wonderful variety of seasonal shows and movies! Pop a big bowl of popcorn, snuggle under a cozy quilt and enjoy a classic Christmas movie with your family...or dress up, invite friends to visit, take pictures, sing carols and watch old, classic Christmas movies. Some great nostalgic holiday videos you won't want to miss are "White Christmas," "Miracle on 34th Street," "The Honeymooners' Christmas," "It's a Wonderful Life," "Meet Me in St. Louis," "A Christmas Carol," "The Judy Garland Christmas Show," "Ed Sullivan's Classic Christmas" and "The Apartment." Delight the kids or relive your own childhood with favorites like "How the Grinch Stole Christmas," "Rudolph, the Red-Nosed Reindeer" or "Merry Christmas Charlie Brown."

"...seek peace and comfort in the joyful simplicities."
— Woman's Home Companion, 1935

Pick an evening for a family "card party." Whip up some special snacks and spend the evening at the kitchen table signing your Christmas cards. Holiday greetings are cherished when they're signed by each family member. Don't forget pets! (Paw print rubber stamps work well for these autographs!) Keep one of your own signed Christmas cards each year in a holiday scrapbook...It's a joy to see the kids' signatures "grow up" over the years.

Invite friends over for an address-the-Christmas-cards party. Ask them to bring a snack to share, along with their cards, stamps, address books and return labels. Try to have this event as early in the season as possible. The week after Thanksgiving would be a good time.

Throw a caroling party! Bring along the words to your favorite carols and visit your neighbors, a nursing home or hospital. End the evening with cocoa and cookies at your home.

Begin a tradition of taking your children to see "The Nutcracker Suite."

Take time out during the busy holiday season...go out to dinner with someone special or have a winter picnic by the fire!

Have friends over for an old-fashioned tree-trimming party! Pull out all your favorite ornaments, have holiday music playing and serve lots of yummy snacks!

Enjoy the delights of winter... wake your family to the smell of sizzling bacon, build a snowman together, take a nap, make a pot of homemade soup.

Set aside one night during the holidays to say "No TV tonight," turn out the lights, tell Christmas stories and "remember when's." Play board games or read aloud.

*Take A Walk on Christmas Eve & Look for the Christmas Star * Visit Your Local Animal Shelter with A Bag of Treats. * Have A Tea Party ~ Family Only! * Buy A Gift for An Elderly Friend & Deliver It with A Hug. * Say A Prayer.

START YouR OWN!

For a cherished tradition, add a new decoration to your ornament collection every year. Instructions for our dated ornament are on page 121.

For a special mother-daughter memory, take an evening for yourselves right before Christmas. Have a leisurely dinner at a favorite restaurant, exchange little gifts, then attend a holiday concert.

Host a Christmas workshop. Set up card tables with rubber stamps, inks, colored pencils, sparkles, scraps of fabrics, ribbon and paints. Have a fun time making cards, gift wrap and ornaments.

Take an annual Christmas hayride with friends and family! Sing carols, visit neighbors and bring a thermos of cocoa to share.

Instead of a sit-down dinner on Christmas Eve, be informal and have yummy appetizers and desserts...much easier to prepare and a very relaxed atmosphere.

Sing a Christmas carol while you're in the shower!

Try keeping a "next year" journal. Tell yourself what to do differently next year, or make lists of places to go, people to see and things to do that you never got to do this year. Review your notes once in a while during the year so you don't forget again next year. You can plan to do a lot more when you know what it is you want to accomplish!

Surprise someone with a kiss under the mistletoe!

Children love traditions too! Make lasting memories by creating magical moments...

Leave a Santa hat by the tree and tell the children, "Oh, my, Santa dropped his hat!" Save it for next year and leave it out so Santa can come back to retrieve his hat.

Make this the year that reindeer start spilling carrot "crumbs" during their midnight visit. Surprise your kids by putting shredded carrots all over the front lawn. Have a camera ready to capture their reactions!

Leave cookies for Santa on a collectible plate. Instructions are on page 122.

Family Collections

Start a family collection... try snowmen, reindeers, santas or angels. Let family members add to it each year. Have a contest for the most original addition!

A holiday collection is like visiting old friends...

...and each time you add to the collection, you add a new memory.

This one is my very favorite!

If you're thinking about starting a family collection, try snowmen... they're fun to collect! The best thing about them is that they get to "hang out" after all the decorations are put away. After all, snowmen aren't just for Christmas! Their smiling faces take the sting out of the task of packing up the Christmas treasures!

Collect poetry and sayings from old Christmas cards. They're perfect if you design your own needlework or greeting cards.

One benefit of having a collection is that everyone will know what to get you for Christmas...Santas, snowmen, teacups or pottery.

Christmas is the time to display your collections. Show off your favorite embroidered linens, bedding and table dressings. Bring out all your very best quilts and layer in chairs, couches, fold on top of cupboards...make your home cozy for the holidays!

If you collect miniatures, you can use your collections to decorate your house for Christmas. For example, if you collect little houses or log cabins, you can place them among fresh greens on top of a mantel or piano. They'll give you so much pleasure when you can share them with family and friends.

Most of us have at least one treasured antique silver serving spoon. Why not display it? Add a tiny bit of greenery and some ribbon to the bottom of the handle, near the bowl. The handles are usually so pretty, and the decorations dress them up even more for the holidays.

A Sprinkle Here, A Sparkle There

Capture the magic of Christmas with cheerful, old-fashioned touches...glowing candles, handmade ornaments, heartwarming gingerbread men and more. On the following pages, you'll find dozens of ways to make your home warm and cozy for the coming season. With the help of Kate, Holly & Mary Elizabeth, you'll discover how to add the personal touch that only you can give...a touch that's sure to wrap up the happiest, most festive holiday season ever.

Enhance the homespun charm of pillars and tapers by arranging them artfully in antique candlesticks, pottery bowls and tins. Add interest by displaying candles of varying heights, or try setting a votive in a hollowed-out apple or orange. Complement with accents like dried fruit and winter greenery.

"The Holly's Up,
The House is All Bright,
The Tree is Ready,
The Candles Alight."
— from an old Christmas Carol

Oh, the warm glow of Candlelight!

Set the scene for an enchanting holiday with candles coated in fragrant spices. Instructions for making these candles are on page 122.

Votives find a natural home inside hollowed-out apples, oranges, grapefruits & lemons.

Ivy, ferns & holly leaves look festive with fat pillar candles. Glue leaves in place and tie with jute or raffia around the middle of the candle.

BAY LEAF VOTIVE

Use a rubber band to fasten fresh glossy bay leaves around a clear glass candleholder. Tie a bow around the middle with gold florist's ribbon.

SANTA CAN CANDLE

Turn an ordinary can into a handmade candle! Fill the can with melted paraffin and allow to cool slightly. Insert a waxed wick; let cool. Paint the can and embellish with ribbon, a cutout from a holiday card and a touch of greenery.

Place a votive on an old-fashioned tin saucer and surround it with peppermint candies...charming!

A joy that's shared is a joy made double!

— English Proverb

ICE CANDLES

To make each candle, cut the top from a clean milk carton to desired height. Use wax stick-ums to secure artificial greenery, pine cones and berries to the inside walls of the carton. (Stick-ums will melt when covered with hot wax.) Melt some wax in a coffee can that has been placed in a pan of water. Stir wax to aid in melting, and heat water to a simmer. Place the carton in a shallow foil-lined pan. Center a taper or votive candle in the carton. Make sure the wick is above the top

of the carton. Fill the remaining area around the candle with ice. (The larger the ice cubes and the more ice you use will result in larger holes in the candle.) Slowly pour melted wax over the ice in the carton. Allow to cool completely and pour off water. To remove from carton, simply tear paper gently away from candle. An ice candle looks beautiful displayed in an antique tin or miniature iron skillet surrounded by greenery.

If you don't have a large holiday budget or are pressed for time, take gold foil stars (the kind that peel off) and stick them on plain white votive candles for quick holiday decorations.

"A bayberry candle burned to the socket brings luck to the house, food to the larder, and gold to the pocket."

— Tomie de Paola

HOMESPUN CANDLES

Here's an easy idea that will add simple holiday charm to your favorite pillar candles. Gather an assortment of homespun fabrics and candles in coordinating Christmas colors. Glue torn strips of fabrics around the candles. Try your hand at layering fabrics, adding buttons or tying the candles with raffia and bows for different looks. These make wonderful accents during the holidays and all year 'round!

STANDING STORYBOOK SANTA

This nostalgic design, pages 142-143, was stitched (omitting the words) over 2 fabric threads on a 20"x32" piece of Ivory Aida (14ct). Seven strands of floss or blending filament were used for Cross Stitches, page 136, and 3 strands for Backstitches, page 136, and French Knots, page 135. Refer to Attaching Beads, page 136, to attach Mill Hill Beads (#05025) using 3 strands of DMC 321 floss.

Centering the design, trim the stitched piece to 13"x24". Cut a 13"x24" piece of Aida for backing and a 9"x8" piece for the base. Matching right sides and raw edges and leaving the bottom edge open for stuffing, sew the stitched piece and the backing together 1/8-inch from the design. Trim the bottom edge of the figure 3/4-inch from the bottom of the design. Leaving a 1/4-inch seam allowance, cut out the figure; clip the curves. Turn the figure right side out and carefully push the curves outward. Press the raw edges at bottom 1/4-inch to the wrong side; stuff the figure with polyester fiberfill to 1 1/2-inches from the opening.

For the base, place the figure on tracing paper; draw around the figure. Add a 1/2-inch seam allowance to the pattern; cut out. Place the pattern on a piece of Aida. Use a fabric marking pencil to draw around the pattern; cut out along the drawn line. Baste around the base piece 1/2-inch from the raw edge; press the raw edges to the wrong side along the basting line.

To weight the bottom of the figure, fill a plastic bag with a small amount of aquarium gravel. Insert the bag into the opening of the figure.

Pin the wrong side of the base piece over the opening. Whipstitch in place, adding fiberfill as necessary. Remove the basting thread.

Santa Claus...just the mention of his name brings a thrill to our hearts! You'll want to add this cross-stitched wall hanging and doll to your collection. Instructions for the wall hanging are on pages 122-123.

Try something different this Christmas. Instead of the traditional stockings hanging on the mantel, line up various sizes and styles of Santa hats to hold Christmas treasures.

Bring the joy of a snowy winter day indoors by accenting your home with reminders of our frosty friends. Instructions for our snowball decorations are on pages 123-124.

Save a snowball in the freezer and in July, get it out and remember all the Christmas fun you had!

Snow BALLS

make great additions to your snowmen displays. Just sprinkle a little pile of artificial snow or glitter & top with a snowball.

FOR A BEAUTIFUL CENTERPIECE

Fill a midnight blue bowl with assorted snowballs entwined with metallic star garlands, and add tiny white lights (battery-operated work best). Add crystal vases filled with twig branches, painted white & sprinkled with glitter, on both sides. Hang tiny snow-flakes or stars from branches. White votive candles on mirrored tiles are the final touch.

SNOWMAN PILLOW

- cotton batting
- paper-backed fusible web
- assorted colors of felt
- black and ivory embroidery floss
- 8½-inch square of green striped fabric
- four large ivory buttons
- polyester fiberfill

Refer to Embroidery Stitches, page 135, and use 3 strands of black embroidery floss for all stitching unless otherwise indicated. Use a ¼-inch seam allowance for all machine stitching.

1. Cut two 13-inch squares from cotton batting.

2. Using patterns, page 141, follow *Making Appliqués, page 134,* to make 2 eyes, 5 squares and one of each remaining appliqué shape from felt or batting. Center and pin a 4¾-inch square of felt on a 5¾-inch square of batting; work Blanket Stitches along the edges of the felt square to secure. Arrange and fuse appliqués on felt square.

3. Work Running Stitches for the mouth and along edges of the nose, stripes on scarf, scarf and hat cuff. Work Blanket Stitches along the edge of the hat, pom-pom and face. Use 2 strands of ivory floss to work a small straight stitch for the highlight in each eye.

4. Press each edge of the fabric square ¼-inch to the wrong side. Center and pin the stitched piece on the fabric. Work a Running Stitch along the edges of the batting to attach to fabric piece.

5. Center the fabric on one 13-inch square; top stitch in place. Using ivory floss, sew a button to each corner of fabric. Place the 13-inch squares right sides together. Leaving an opening for turning, sew the squares together.

6. Turn the pillow right side out and stuff with fiberfill; sew the opening closed.

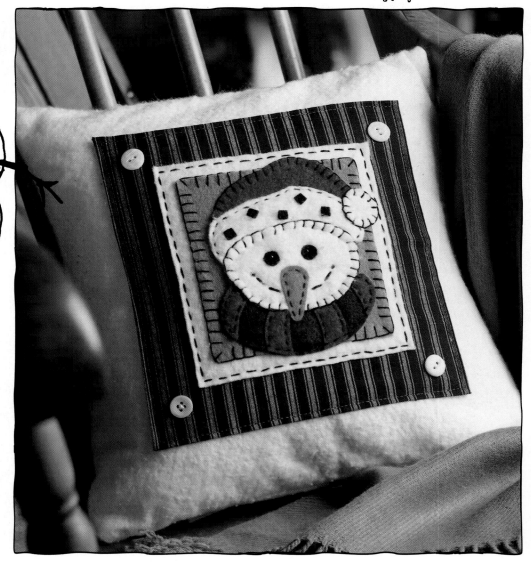

Let our fun-loving snow pals brighten your holiday decor. The snuggly snowman pillow adds a friendly touch to any corner, and the snowmen jars are lighted from the inside with Christmas bulbs.

26

LIGHTED SNOW FAMILY

There's no better way to light up your holidays than to make a lighted snowman for each member of your family; use assorted sizes of jars. Sponge paint the outside of the jars white; let dry. Use dimensional paint to add eyes, mouth, buttons and a carrot nose; let dry. Cut a one inch dia. hole in the center of each jar lid; place the lids on the jars. The next part is kinda tricky...you'll need a string of 5-watt, cool burning, clip-on lights with one bulb for each jar (if you have extra lights you'll need to tuck them away in your display). Insert a light in each hole and secure with electrical tape...make sure the wires are taped to the back of the jar. For the hats, cover each lid with a pinked circle of felt and tie with a strip of homespun. On our little fellow, we added circles of felt for earmuffs and a felt cuff around his hat. Embellish the hats with greenery, then tie a homespun scarf around each snow family member.

*S*prigs of Queen Anne's lace look like snowflakes when tucked in the branches of a small tree.

Easy Kitchen Decorating Ideas

Make your kitchen merry and bright for Christmas. Sweet gingerbread, fragrant fruit, snowy white popcorn... the decorations will smell as wonderful as they look!

Cover a wreath and tabletop tree with your favorite country kitchen goodies. We used gingerbread men, kitchen utensils, homespun bows and dried fruit for an old-fashioned feel. Instructions for these decorations are on page 124.

NOTHING SAYS *Welcome* LIKE A WREATH ON THE DOOR!

A small kitchen tree is perfect for displaying your collection of spoons or cookie cutters...
tie them on with a homespun bow. Or decorate your tree in red...with crimson apples, a
cranberry garland and gingham bows. Another variation is to accent the tree with
fragrant herb bundles, dried flowers and baby's breath with silk ribbons.

Create a Christmasy corner in your country kitchen with an assortment of baskets, pottery, glass jars and antique utensils. Then turn your imagination loose by accenting them with candles, cookbooks, homespun tea towels, dried florals and edibles like popcorn and fruit.

Deck the Walls!

TEA TOWELS

- cotton homespun tea towels
- floss
- paper-backed fusible web
- buttons (optional)
- scraps of fabric for designs

1. Preshrink cotton towels and fabric by washing several times in warm water and mild soap. Dry thoroughly and press.

2. Trace star or snowman designs, page 141, onto paper side of fusible web. Leave a 1/2-inch border around the designs when cutting out.

3. Fuse designs to wrong side of fabrics following the instructions included with fusible webbing. Cut out designs along the drawn lines.

4. Peel off paper backing from designs...place in desired location on towel. Using a pressing cloth to protect your iron, fuse designs in place. Finish edges with a zig-zag machine stitch and primitive hand-stitching. Embellish with buttons to complete.

Perk up your kitchen...tuck a holiday tea towel in a treat basket and give one to your country friends!

Tie cookies to an evergreen rope for a **garland** that smells wonderful and tastes great! ★

Wrap a gift in plain brown kraft paper and tie on a gingerbread tag with gingham rag.

The goodness of holiday foods...bright cranberries, gingerbread men, cinnamon sticks and rosy red apples add appealing aroma and color to a cozy kitchen. Arrange these items in a wooden bowl accented with greenery, in canning jars highlighted with tiny battery-operated lights, or combine them with homespun bows on a heart-shaped grapevine wreath.

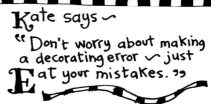

Kate says ~
"Don't worry about making a decorating error ~ just Eat your mistakes."

33

Hang a Stocking

... on the mantel

or on the back of a chair,
on the bedroom doorknob
~or~
just anywhere!

PRIMITIVE STOCKINGS

These hand-stitched stockings will add loads of homemade charm to your mantel this season! Gather an assortment of fabrics such as tea-dyed canvas, wool or burlap. Follow *Making Patterns*, page 134, to trace our Stocking Top and Bottom patterns, page 145, onto tracing paper. Fold fabric in half. Cutting ¼-inch outside the pattern edge, cut out the 2 stocking pieces. Trace your favorite design, pages 144 and 145, onto tracing paper and pin to the front of one stocking piece. Refer to *Embroidery Stitches*, page 135, and use 3 strands of floss to embroider the design; carefully tear away the tracing paper. Matching right sides, leaving the top edge open and using a ¼-inch seam allowance for all sewing, sew the stocking pieces together. Clip the curves and turn the stocking right side out. For the cuff, match right sides and sew the short ends of a 14"x3½" piece of fabric together. Matching wrong sides and raw edges, press the cuff in half. Matching the raw edge of the cuff to the top edge of the stocking and cuff seam to heel seam, place the cuff over the stocking; sew cuff and stocking together. Pull the cuff upright and press. For the hanger, knot the ends of a 5-inch length of jute together; tack the knot at the inside cuff seam.

For an aromatic country touch, fill stockings or mittens with sprigs of greenery and cinnamon sticks.

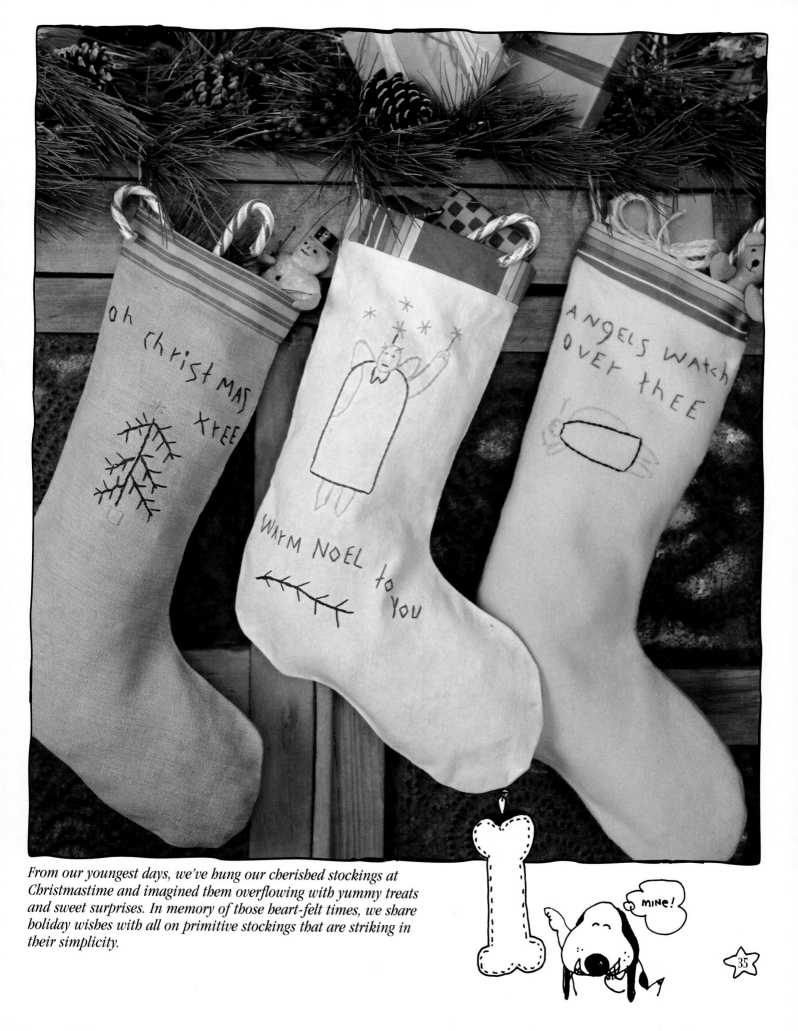

From our youngest days, we've hung our cherished stockings at Christmastime and imagined them overflowing with yummy treats and sweet surprises. In memory of those heart-felt times, we share holiday wishes with all on primitive stockings that are striking in their simplicity.

ORNAMENTS

(Use your cookie cutters for great patterns)

ORNAMENTS

YOU WILL NEED:

★ COOKIE CUTTERS
★ FELT SHEETS
★ EMBROIDERY FLOSS
★ NEEDLE

1. TRACE AROUND EACH COOKIE CUTTER TWICE ON FELT; CUT OUT SHAPES.

2. STITCH THE TWO FELT PIECES TOGETHER USING A RUNNING STITCH & THREE STRANDS OF FLOSS.

3. MAKE A FLOSS LOOP FOR HANGING.

Easy!

★ Embellish your work with buttons, fancy stitches, sequins, seed pearls or beads!

Felt ornaments in cookie cutter shapes add soft warmth to your holiday decor. Instructions for the ornaments in the photograph are on pages 124-125.

A-gathering We shall go

Twig Stars

...NATURALLY BEAUTIFUL!

YOU WILL NEED:

★ 5 TWIGS OF EQUAL LENGTH
★ HOT GLUE OR THICK CRAFT GLUE
★ THIN TWINE OR JUTE ~ OPTIONAL

—★—

1. MAKE AN UPSIDE-DOWN "V" SHAPE WITH 2 TWIGS. GLUE TO SECURE IN PLACE.

2. GLUE THIRD STICK ACROSS UPPER PORTION OF TRIANGLE.

3. GLUE REMAINING STICKS INTO PLACE AS SHOWN.

4. WHEN GLUE HAS SET, ADD GREENERY, BUTTONS, BELLS OR HOMESPUN BOWS FOR A RUSTIC LOOK.

TWIG FRAME

Has your collection of old Christmas cards begun to overflow? Try this simple idea to revive one of your favorites and add a bit of country charm to a mantel or bedside table. Center and glue a card in the opening of a precut photo mat. Draw around the mat on a piece of cardboard; cut out and glue to the back of the mat. For the stand, cut a 1½-inch wide cardboard strip the height of the frame. Bend the stand one inch from the top; glue the top section to the center top edge on the back of the frame. For stability, glue a length of ribbon between the frame and stand. Glue twigs over the entire mat. Embellish with a gingham bow, a gold wooden star and greenery for a festive reminder of holidays past!

HOLLY'S PINECONE Topiaries

Go on a winter's day hike ᔫ and come back with enough pine cones for a collection of topiaries! They look wonderful marching across a mantel or windowsill, or make extras for holiday gift-giving.

You'll Need:

- PINE CONES
- CLAY POTS
- CINNAMON STICKS OR TWIGS
- MOSS
- PIECES OF FLORAL FOAM
- PLASTER·OF·PARIS
- HOT GLUE
- SCRAPS OF HOMESPUN
- NATURAL RAFFIA

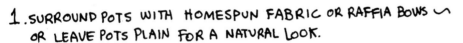

1. SURROUND POTS WITH HOMESPUN FABRIC OR RAFFIA BOWS ᔫ OR LEAVE POTS PLAIN FOR A NATURAL LOOK.

2. PLACE SMALL WEDGES OF FOAM IN POTS ᔫ FILL WITH FAIRLY THICK MIXTURE OF PLASTER-OF-PARIS. PLACE TWIGS OR CINNAMON STICKS IN CENTER OF POTS BEFORE PLASTER HARDENS. THE STICKS SHOULD NOT BE LONGER THAN TWO TIMES POT'S HEIGHT.

3. AFTER PLASTER HARDENS, COVER WITH MOSS FOR A FINISHED LOOK.

4. GLUE PINE CONES TO TOPS OF STICKS.

* HOLLY'S HINT: "EMBELLISH YOUR CREATION WITH RIBBON OR RAFFIA BOWS, A SPRINKLE OF GLITTER OR GOLD PAINT. TUCK IN A FEW TINY PINE CONES AROUND THE STICK'S BASE."

The very name of Christmas ᔫ All that's merry, sweet and gay ᔫ and may it bring the very thing ᔫ you long for most this happy day.
~FROM AN ANTIQUE POSTCARD ᔫ

Whether displayed alone or in groups, pine cone topiaries in pots covered with homespun fabrics, torn fabric bows and raffia accents add a festive touch to your decor. Instructions for making the large topiary, which includes acorns, nuts and sweet gum balls, are on page 125.

GRAPEVINE CENTERPIECE AND KISSING BALL

Gather up any spare grapevine you may have around. Soak the grapevine in warm water until pliable. Using a large round balloon that is inflated, gently wrap the grapevine around the balloon to form a sphere. Make it as dense or as sparse as you like. Once the grapevine has dried, pop the balloon. These spheres make a magical **Centerpiece** (facing page) when wired with tiny white lights and arranged in a basket with bright red bows and sprigs of evergreen! You can also shape a dainty **Kissing Ball** (above) using a small balloon. Form a hanging loop from jute and embellish with holly, mistletoe and a homespun bow...hang it in the nearest doorway and steal a kiss from your Christmas sweetie!

the best things in life are free.

OLD SAYING

TWIGGY TREE

* THICK JUTE
* 12 TWIGS, RANGING IN SIZE FROM 1" TO 8"
* HOT GLUE OR THICK CRAFT GLUE
* PAINTED OR NATURAL WOODEN STAR
* SHORT THICK TWIG FOR TRUNK

① CUT A PIECE OF JUTE 9" LONG. MEASURE DOWN ON JUTE 2" & BEGIN GLUING TWIGS AT THAT POINT. START WITH SHORTEST TWIG & FINISH WITH LONGEST.

② FOLD A 4" PIECE OF JUTE ON TOP INTO A LOOP ~ SECURE WITH GLUE TO TOP OF JUTE. GLUE STAR ON TOP OF TREE TO HIDE LOOP ENDING.

③ TRIM EXCESS JUTE FROM BOTTOM OF TREE ~ GLUE ON TRUNK. LET DRY COMPLETELY BEFORE HANGING.

KATE'S TIP: DO NOT HOT GLUE FINGERS TO ANY CRAFT PROJECT.

Create a simple centerpiece from a circle of mistletoe loosely wrapped in ribbon. Tuck a pillar candle in the middle.

43

Angels on High

Share news of peace and goodwill with country angels. Outline a childlike drawing with embroidery stitches, then display in a frame or stuff to make tree ornaments. Instructions are on pages 125-126.

A simple arrangement of long-needle pine, old-fashioned ornaments and cinnamon sticks looks beautiful set on a sideboard.

Make personalized ornaments for everyone in your family! Use paint to write names and draw designs on glass balls, then glue on jewels, sequins or beads. Add a big bow to the top of the ball. Be sure to make new ornaments for new family members. It's a great way to welcome a new son or daughter-in-law...or baby!...to the family.

Snowed In

Fill a pair of mittens with potpourri. Join the mittens with a string of yarn, then hang them from a peg near your door for a cozy seasonal look and a holiday scent.

MITTEN GARLAND

- tracing paper
- scraps of homespun
- cotton batting
- felt
- fabric glue
- black embroidery floss
- old sweaters
- assorted buttons
- polyester fiberfill
- scraps of lace
- jute twine
- jute rope

Refer to Embroidery Stitches, page 135, and use 3 strands of floss unless otherwise indicated. Apply glue to cut edges of sweater pieces to prevent unravelling; allow to dry.

Our sweet mitten swag will bring an old-fashioned feel to your holiday decorations. Cut simple shapes from colorful felt or old sweaters and embellish with lace, buttons and appliqués.

Trace desired patterns, page 147, onto tracing paper; cut out. For each felt or batting mitten, use the patterns and cut 2 of each mitten shape and one of each appliqué from materials. Glue desired appliqués to one mitten shape (this will be the front), then work stitches along the edge of each appliqué. Place the mitten front and back wrong sides together. Leaving the top edge open for stuffing, work desired stitches along the outer edge to close.

For each sweater mitten, turn a sweater inside out and pin the front and back together with ribbed edges even. Pin one mitten pattern to the sweater and draw around the edge. Leaving the top edge open

for stuffing, sew along the drawn line; cut out 1/4-inch outside the sewn line. Turn the mitten right side out; embellish one side with buttons.

Stuff each mitten with fiberfill. For a fancy cuff, glue a scrap of lace or leftover sweater cuff around the top edge of your mitten. For the hanger, cut a 4-inch length of twine or 1/2"x4" strip from felt or sweater scraps; fold in half. Glue or stitch the hanger ends to the cuff of each mitten. Glue the opening closed. Thread hangers onto a length of rope; glue in place. Knot the rope at each end. Tie torn strips of homespun into bows and glue to rope between mittens; glue a button to the center of each bow.

ALL THROUGH THE HOUSE

COUNTRY · FRIEND · IDEAS · FOR · CHRISTMAS

*From dining room to guest room and all in between...
make your house a merry celebration of the season! Create
a festive welcome with our painted floorcloth.*

STOCKING UP:

TEA·DYE REGULAR OLD GYM SOCKS (RED·BANDED ONES LOOK NEAT) UNTIL THEY'RE VERY DARK... BEAT 'EM UP REAL GOOD ... WEAR A FEW HOLES IN 'EM ... RUN OVER THEM A COUPLE OF TIMES... STRETCH 'EM... WONDERFUL <u>PRIMITIVE</u> STOCKINGS TO HANG ON A DOOR, WREATH OR GATE, FILLED WITH GREENERY & CANDY CANES.

NO PLACE TO HANG A STOCKING?

TEA·DYE, EMBROIDER OR RUBBER·STAMP A PILLOWCASE WITH YOUR NAME & A CHRISTMAS DESIGN. ATTACH WITH A RIBBON TO YOUR BED·POST! (GOOD FOR EXTRA·BIG STOCKING STUFFERS)

KEEP HOLIDAY NOTEPADS HANDY FOR CHRISTMAS LISTS & DOODLES.

FILL A WATERING CAN WITH AN EVERGREEN BOUGH FOR A PORCH DECORATION.

FLOOR CLOTH

- yardstick
- pencil
- 30"x40" canvas floor cloth
- compressed craft sponge
- red, light green, green, light brown and brown acrylic paint
- paintbrushes
- natural sponge
- tracing paper
- transfer paper
- spray sealer

Refer to Painting Techniques and Making Patterns, page 134, for hints from your Country Friends®. Allow paint and sealer to dry after each application.

1. Use the yardstick and pencil to lightly draw a line one inch inside each edge of the floor cloth.

2. Cut a one inch square from craft sponge.

3. Following the drawn lines, use the craft sponge to paint a red checkerboard pattern around the edges of the floor cloth. Use the tip of a paintbrush handle and light green paint to paint a dot in the center of each square.

4. Trace patterns, pages 148-149, onto tracing paper. Use transfer paper to transfer tree designs to the floor cloth.

5. Paint the tree sections green; use the natural sponge to highlight with light green paint. Paint the tree trunks brown and use light brown paint to highlight.

6. Spray the finished floor cloth with 2 coats of sealer.

7. Store the floor cloth flat or roll with the design to the inside; clean gently with a damp cloth as needed.

"When love adorns a home, other ornaments are secondary."
— *Anonymous*

STRING Red JINGLE BELLS ON PLAIN OLD TWINE and HANG ACROSS WINDOWS & DOORS, TIE UP PACKAGES WITH IT OR WEAR IT AS A NECKLACE!

SMELLS WONDERFUL!

FOR **Friends**

CHRISTMAS BALSAM POTPOURRI SACHETS

In the language of herbs, balsam stands for *Warm Friendship*. Send a little reminder of that home with your guests with these fragrant sachets!

- 2 c. dried balsam fir needles
- ¼ c. dried orange or lemon peel
- 1 T. cedar chips
- 1 t. whole cloves
- 1 t. whole allspice
- 1 to 2 drops of evergreen or bayberry oil

Mix all ingredients in a wide mouth mason jar. Cover ~ let cure 4 to 6 weeks. Shake gently once or twice a week.

Sachets:

- 5"x16" piece of holiday print fabric
- ½ c. balsam mix
- ribbon
- preserved cedar, dried flowers or dried pepperberries
- hot glue gun

Fold fabric in half with right sides together. Sew side seams ~ turn right side out. Turn down top edge (about 2") to bag's inside ~ press to finish top of bag. Fill with potpourri. Tie closed ~ use glue gun to affix cedar & berries to bag for decoration.

ROUND DOILY SACHET

- tea bag
- two 8-inch dia. doilies
- embroidery floss
- potpourri
- assorted buttons
- two 18-inch lengths of ⅛-inch wide ribbon

Refer to Embroidery Stitches, page 135, and use 6 strands of embroidery floss for all stitching unless otherwise indicated.

1. Refer to Tea Dyeing, page 134, to dye doilies.

2. Use Running Stitches to work the word "Peace" on the front of one doily. Pin the doilies wrong sides together. Fold the top edges down 2½-inches for flaps. Leaving the top edges open for stuffing, work Running Stitches along the bottom edge to form a pocket.

3. Lightly stuff the sachet with potpourri.

4. Stitching through all layers and knotting the ends at the front, sew buttons along the front edge of the flap. Use floss to tie buttons along the bottom edge of the sachet.

5. Thread a length of ribbon through the fold of each flap; loosely gather the top. Knot the ribbons together on each side to secure the gathers. Knot the ribbon ends together if desired.

(continued on page 126)

Cranberries, an old holiday tradition, can be used to decorate wreaths and topiaries too! Simply string them on floral wire and the strands can be used in arrangements and bent to fit any design.

HOMESPUN WREATH

- 5 assorted 22"x3" strips of torn homespun
- hot glue gun
- cedar and pine sprigs
- dried orange slices
- canella berries
- pine cones
- 24-inch dia. fresh evergreen wreath
- floral wire

1. Arrange cedar and pine sprigs, orange slices, canella berries and pine cones on the wreath and glue in place.

2. Tie fabric strips into bows.

3. Insert a 12-inch length of wire through the back of the knot on each bow; use to secure the bows to the wreath.

OH, CHRISTMAS TREE

Let your tree shine with festive spirit from top to bottom!
Santa's the star of the show at the tip of the tree, and jingling
appliqués twinkle on the scalloped skirt. Instructions
for the tree topper and skirt are on pages 126-127.

When trimming your holiday tree, use garland or ribbon to divide the tree lengthwise into sections. Each member of the family gets their own section to decorate. Children especially love this tradition, and look forward to decorating their own special section each year.

Kids' Holiday Table

Get all the kids together for a Christmas crafts party...include the cousins, grandchildren and neighborhood friends. They'll have a ball decorating a tablecloth and adding their names, and you'll have a memory to cherish! For take-home favors, show them how to make funny-face reindeer out of tiny flowerpots.

You'll Need:
- ★ A BLANK WHITE TABLECLOTH (MAKE YOUR OWN OR BUY A FINISHED PLAIN CLOTH)
- ★ CRAYONS, FABRIC OR PERMANENT MARKERS
- ★ SEVERAL KIDS WITH BIG IMAGINATIONS
- ★ RED OR GREEN EMBROIDERY FLOSS

HOW TO:

1.

Cover table with newspaper. Spread out cloth; use masking tape to hold in place.

2.

With crayons or markers, let children trace their hands ∽ add name and year in center of hands ∽ decorate handprints like gloves. Let them draw their favorite holiday items: Christmas trees, snowmen, candy canes, stars, Santa, etc.

3.

Finish edge of tablecloth with cheery embroidery floss using a blanket stitch. An older child (with a little help) can master this stitch with ease.

"It is good to be children sometimes, and never better than at Christmas."

— Charles Dickens

ARE THOSE KIDS STILL HERE?

REINDEER ORNAMENT

Here's a project the whole family can share! Simply trace around the rim of a 2½-inch high clay pot on a piece of cardboard; cut out just inside the drawn line. Punch 2 small holes, one inch apart, in the center of the cardboard. Glue 2 wiggle eyes to the side of the pot just beneath the rim. For the nose, glue a miniature red Christmas ball in the hole in the bottom of the pot. Use a black fine-point marker to draw eyebrows and a mouth on the reindeer. Glue twigs to the rim of the pot for antlers. Glue several pieces of raffia between the antlers for hair; tie a scrap of ribbon into a small bow and glue to raffia. To finish, thread a length of floral wire through the holes in the cardboard circle. With the wire ends extending outward, glue the cardboard to the rim of the pot. Use the wires to secure your reindeer to the tree.

Now, doesn't this look like **FUN?**

55

Make it merry, Wrap it bright

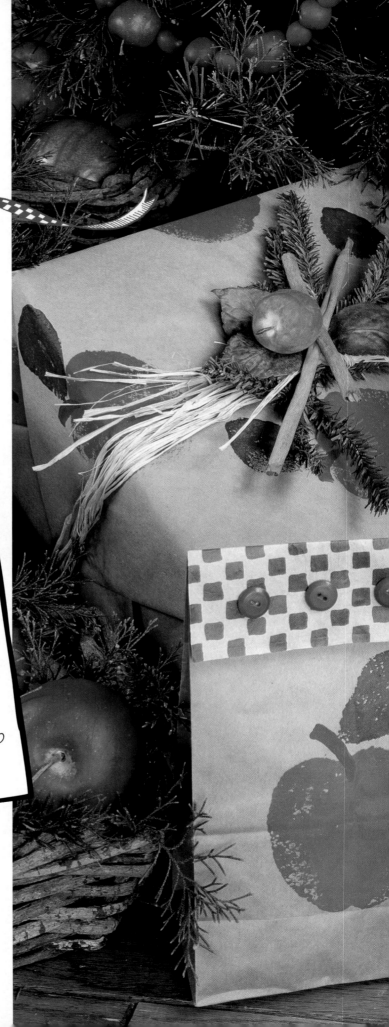

To Holly From Kate

Take a hint from Kate, Holly & Mary Elizabeth...the very best gifts are handmade from the heart! Fill a basket with decorated soaps or make folky bookmarks for nice little gifts, decorate a cardigan and mittens for a family member or crochet an afghan for a special friend. Be sure your packages are merry and bright, too! Make your own gift wrap and cards to send your best holiday wishes.

Don't wrap your handmade, one-of-a-kind gifts in store-bought paper...create packages that are as special as the treats inside! Instructions for the apple-stamped gift wrap, bags, and card are on page 127.

Love is an excess of friendship.
-ARISTOTLE-

what better time of year to tell those you love just how important they are to you? Write a short (or long!) letter and tuck it inside your Christmas card — it's a gift they won't forget.

Dear Friend,
Holly

Kate

The whimsical illustrations on these stationery sets and greeting cards are easy to create...just photocopy our designs and shade using colored pencils. Instructions for the stationery sets are on page 128.

CHRISTMAS CARDS

Delight a friend or loved one with a handmade Christmas card this year! Begin with an assortment of purchased cards. Use decorative-edge or straight-edge scissors to cut a piece of fabric or corrugated cardboard slightly smaller than the front of the card; glue to front of card. Use colored pencils to color a photocopy of your favorite design, page 152, then use a black permanent marker to add a greeting. Trim the design and glue to the front of the card. Use greenery, buttons or jute bows to embellish your card. And don't forget...if you plan to mail your card, remember to mark the envelope "Hand Cancel!"

A great way to avoid those crazy, stressful shopping malls during the holidays is to give homemade coupons. Fun to give as well as receive, coupons for cleaning someone's house, cooking a meal, watering their plants, giving a perm, grocery shopping, baking a pie or walking the dog are always welcomed. Kids love making their very own coupons too!

A Cozy Country Christmas

Spread the holiday spirit by sharing a gift that warms both body and soul.
Highlighted with bright bows, this cozy afghan is an impressive way to show you care.

CHRISTMAS TREE COVERLET

Finished Size: 45"x66"

MATERIALS

Red Heart® Worsted Weight Yarn
[3 ounces (170 yards) per skein]:
Aran - 9 skeins
Dark Spruce - 8 skeins
Burgundy - 1 skein
Crochet hook, size G (4.00 mm) **or** size
needed for gauge
Yarn needle

GAUGE: Each Strip = 5¹⁄₂-inches wide and
Each repeat = 4-inches

*Refer to Crochet, page 136, for abbreviations
and general instructions.*

STRIP (Make 8)

FOUNDATION

♥With Dark Spruce, ch 210 **loosely**.

♥**First Side** (Right side): Sc in second ch from
hook and in next ch, ★ † hdc in next 2 chs, dc in
next 2 chs, tr in next 2 chs, dtr in next ch,
(dtr, ch 4, slip st) in next ch †, slip st in next
4 chs, sc in next 2 chs; repeat from ★ 13 times
more, then repeat from † to † once, slip st in
last 3 chs; do **not** finish off: 284 sts.

Note: Mark last stitch on First Side as **right** side
and bottom edge.

♥**Second Side:** Ch 2, working in free loops of
beginning ch, slip st in same ch and in next 2 chs,
★ † (slip st, ch 4, dtr) in next ch, dtr in next ch,
tr in next 2 chs, dc in next 2 chs, hdc in next
2 chs †, sc in next 2 chs, slip st in next 4 chs;
repeat from ★ 13 times **more**, then repeat from
† to † once, sc in next ch, 2 sc in next ch (same
ch as first sc on First Side); join with slip st to first
sc on First Side, do **not** finish off: 569 sts and one
ch-2 sp on First and Second Sides.

BORDER

♥**Rnd 1:** Ch 1, sc in same st and in next 9 sts, 2 sc
in next ch, slip st in next 3 chs, ★ skip next slip st,
slip st in next 4 slip sts, sc in next 10 sts, 2 sc in
next ch, slip st in next 3 chs; repeat from
★ 13 times **more**, skip next slip st, slip st in next
3 slip sts, 4 sc in next ch-2 sp, slip st in next
3 slip sts, skip next slip st, slip st in next 3 chs,
2 sc in next ch, place marker around last sc made for
st placement, sc in next 10 sts, † slip st in next
4 slip sts, skip next slip st, slip st in next 3 chs,
2 sc in next ch, sc in next 10 sts †, repeat from † to †
across to last sc, 3 sc in last sc; join with slip st to
first sc, finish off: 575 sts.

♥**Rnd 2:** With **right** side facing, join Aran with
slip st in marked sc; slip st in next sc, sc in next
2 sc, hdc in next 2 sc, dc in next 2 sc, tr in next
4 sts, ★ dtr in next 3 slip sts, skip next 4 sts,
slip st in next 2 sc, sc in next 2 sc, hdc in next 2 sc,
dc in next 2 sc, tr in next 4 sts; repeat from
★ 13 times **more**, dtr in next sc, (dtr, ch 5, sc, ch 5,
dtr) in next sc, dtr in joining slip st, tr in same sc
joining slip st is worked into, tr in next 3 sc, dc in next
2 sc, hdc in next 2 sc, sc in next 2 sc, slip st in next
2 sc, † skip next 4 slip sts, dtr in next 3 slip sts, tr in
next 4 sc, dc in next 2 sc, hdc in next 2 sc, sc in next
2 sc, slip st in next 2 sc †, repeat from † to †
13 times **more**, skip next 4 slip sts, dtr in next 4 sts,
(dtr, ch 5, sc, ch 5 dtr) in next sc, dtr in next 4 sts,
skip last 4 sts; join with slip st to first slip st:
480 sts.

♥**Rnd 3:** Ch 1, sc in same st and in each st across
to next ch-5, 3 sc in next ch, sc in next 9 sts, 3 sc
in next ch, sc in each st across to next ch-5, 3 sc in
next ch, sc in next 9 sts, 3 sc in next ch, sc in last
5 dtr; join with slip st to first sc: 488 sc.

♥**Rnd 4:** Ch 3 (**counts as first dc**), dc in next sc
and in each sc around working (2 dc, ch 1, 2 dc) in
center sc of each corner 3-sc group; join with slip st
to first dc, finish off: 500 dc and 4 ch-1 sps.

(continued on page 128)

Let your child wrap gifts this year. So what
if they're not exactly the way you
would have wrapped them...
Grandma will be delighted anyway!

Gifts in a Twinkling

Need some holiday gifts that you can craft in a twinkling?
Creative friends will love a pretty basket of sponge-painted
napkins, a tart pan pincushion or a nostalgic sewing basket.

STAMPED NAPKINS

Here's a quick and easy gift idea for those hard-to-shop-for friends and neighbors.
Purchase a set of napkins. Trace our holly leaf pattern, page 142, onto tracing paper
and cut out. Draw around the pattern on a compressed craft sponge and cut out.
Dip the dampened sponge in green acrylic paint and stamp 2 leaves on one corner of
each napkin; allow the paint to dry. Use a black permanent marker to draw a dashed
line down the center of each leaf. Sew on red buttons for bright berries. Finish your
gift by tying each napkin with raffia and arranging them in a basket decorated with a
handmade tag and a cheerful homespun bow.

To make a gift in a jiffy, craft a cookie cutter wreath! Arrange
cutters in a circle, with edges touching, and glue in place.

BUTTON BASKET

- small basket (ours measures 3-inches high and 13-inches around)
- homespun fabric (we used a 13-inch square)
- batting
- embroidery floss
- buttons
- jute
- hot glue gun

1. Making sure you have plenty of cutting room around the edge, draw around the bottom of the basket on the wrong side of fabric. Measure the height of the basket. Cutting outside the drawn line, cut out the fabric circle the height measurement plus one inch.

2. Using your fabric circle as a pattern, cut out a piece of batting. Trim 1/2-inch off the edge of the batting.

3. Using floss, work *Running Stitches*, page 135, along the edge of the fabric circle. Center the batting, then the basket on the wrong side of the fabric. Pull ends of floss to gather the fabric around the basket just below the top rim. Knot the ends to secure.

4. Glue buttons around the rim of the basket and tie a length of jute over the gathers of the fabric.

TART PAN PINCUSHION

- 3¹/₄-inch dia. tart pan
- scraps of muslin and 2 homespun fabrics
- drawing compass
- scrap of lace
- buttons
- embroidery floss
- polyester fiberfill
- hot glue gun

HEY— NO SHAKING OR PEEKING ALLOWED!

1. Matching right sides and piecing as desired, sew fabrics together to form a 9-inch square. Use the compass to draw a 6¹/₄-inch dia. circle on the wrong side of the fabric square; cut out.

2. Use lace, buttons and *Embroidery Stitches*, page 135, to embellish the circle.

3. Use floss to work a Running Stitch around the edge of the circle. Leaving an opening for stuffing, pull the ends of the floss to gather the fabric; stuff with fiberfill until firm. Pull ends of floss to close the opening; knot to secure.

4. Glue the pincushion in the tart pan.

The best gifts come in small packages...bookmarks for someone who loves to read, or a small basket filled with decorated soaps, an appliquéd towel and other comforts for the bath. Instructions for the bookmarks are on page 133.

HOMEMADE HOLIDAY HAND TOWEL

- hand towel
- homespun fabric for trim
- paper-backed fusible web
- pinking shears
- embroidery floss
- scraps of fabrics for appliqués
- 5 red buttons

Refer to Embroidery Stitches, page 135, and use 3 strands of floss for all stitching.

1. For the trim, measure the width of the towel and add 2 inches. Cut one strip each of homespun and web 1¼-inches wide by the determined measurement; fuse together. Use pinking shears to trim the long edges.

2. Wrapping the ends around sides, center and fuse the strip across the towel. Work Running Stitches along the edges to secure.

3. Using patterns, page 139, follow *Making Appliqués, page 134,* to make bell and leaf appliqués. Center and fuse the appliqués on the towel.

4. Work Blanket Stitches along the edges of each bell and Running Stitches down the center of each leaf. Sew buttons to the towel for berries and clappers.

Neat!

FESTIVE Decorated SOAPS

Kate loves stars, so Mary Elizabeth gave her a basket-full of these wonderful bars along with a star-covered "Holiday Homemade Tea Towel"... a great country gift!

★ SMALL SOAPS
★ HOLIDAY PICTURES CUT FROM GREETING CARDS, WRAPPING PAPER OR STICKERS
★ PARAFFIN   ★ T-PINS
★ CRAFT GLUE   ★ PIE TIN

1. USE SOAPS THAT ARE SMOOTH ~ ROUND & OVALS ARE NICE. ADHERE PICTURES TO SOAPS WITH CRAFT GLUE. LET DRY.

2. USING A PIE TIN IN AN ELECTRIC SKILLET WITH WATER, MELT PARAFFIN OVER LOW HEAT. STICK A PIN IN EACH SIDE OF SOAP FOR HANDLES. WORKING QUICKLY, DIP PICTURE SIDE OF SOAP INTO MELTED PARAFFIN. IT WILL TAKE TWO COATS TO SUCCESSFULLY COVER THE PICTURE. ALLOW PARAFFIN TO DRY BETWEEN COATS.

Jolly Good Gifts

What great gift ideas! Discover how fun and easy it is to add felt appliqués to store-bought fleece mittens and turn bits and pieces of pretty scraps into attractive holiday pins. Instructions for the mittens are on page 129.

SNOWMAN PIN

- 3"x4" piece of muslin
- needle and thread
- polyester fiberfill
- ecru embroidery floss
- craft glue
- 2 small twigs for arms
- orange paint
- toothpick
- black permanent pen
- scraps of fabric
- old knit glove
- pin back
- small button
- greenery

1. For the body, sew the long edges of muslin together. Use floss to tightly tie one end of tube closed. Turn right side out.

2. Stuff tube with fiberfill and tie top end closed.

3. Knotting ends at seam, tie floss around snowman to form body sections.

4. For hat, cut 2-inches from one fingertip of glove. Fold cut edge up to form cuff. Glue hat to head and allow to dry.

5. Use a black pen to draw dots for eyes, mouth and buttons on snowman.

6. Make a small hole in each side of body for arms and another hole in face for nose.

(continued on page 129)

HOMESPUN TREE PIN

- cinnamon stick
- 1/2"x6" torn strips of homespun in shades of green
- light yellow paint
- star-shaped wooden cutout
- corrugated craft cardboard
- 1/8-inch dia. hole punch
- jute
- pin back
- hot glue gun

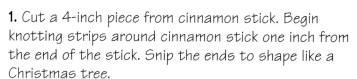

1. Cut a 4-inch piece from cinnamon stick. Begin knotting strips around cinnamon stick one inch from the end of the stick. Snip the ends to shape like a Christmas tree.

2. Paint wooden star yellow; let dry. Glue to top of tree. Glue pin back to back of tree.

3. Cut a 3 1/2"x5" piece from cardboard. Punch 2 holes 3/4-inch apart at center top. Tie a 12-inch length of jute into a bow through holes.

4. Center and press the pin vertically on the cardboard; cut open along indention. Insert pin back through the opening to secure.

Tiny mittens or toddler socks look wonderful framed as a gift for grandparents, or for the child they belonged to once upon a time.

Make your gifts especially heartwarming...knit woolly toboggans for each member of the family, or add country appliqués to a sweatshirt cardigan. Instructions are on pages 129-130.

For a unique gift that can be assembled quickly, partially fill a small galvanized bucket with pebbles. Tuck in flower bulbs and water to cover the pebbles...in no time you'll have blooming flowers in winter!

Wrap it up!

PAPER IDEAS:

KRAFT PAPER

BANDANAS OR FABRICS

TISSUE PAPER

CLOTH OR PAPER NAPKINS

CORRUGATED CARDBOARD

to Meg

FOIL

NEWSPAPER

PAPER BAGS

COMICS

DISH TOWELS

...and of course, regular old WRAPPING PAPER!

Trimmings:

RIBBON

ORNAMENTS

HOMESPUN FABRIC CUT INTO TIES

RAFFIA

STICKERS

PEPPERBERRIES OR CANELLA BERRIES

CRAFT FOAM

PRESERVED GREENERY

BAY LEAVES & HERBS

METALLIC CORD

SHOELACES

CROCHETED OR PAPER DOILIES

CANDY CANES

SPARKLY STAR GARLAND

STRANDS OF FAUX PEARLS

TWIGS

CINNAMON STICKS

DRIED CITRUS SLICES

YARN

Make your Own Gift Wrap!

GOOD STUFF TO USE WHEN YOU MAKE GIFT WRAP

SPRAY PAINTS

OLD TOOTHBRUSH FOR SPATTERING PAINT

FUN SHAPES CUT FROM SPONGES

ACRYLIC PAINTS

RUBBER STAMPS

MARKERS

GLASS JARS & LABELS

Lovely Lacy Giftwrap
...simple & pretty!

PAPER
FANCY PAPER DOILIES
SPRAY PAINT
GLUE STICK OR STRAIGHT PINS

1. Cover work surface with newspapers.

2. Lay paper out on prepared work surface.

3. Place paper doilies on paper as desired. Use a dab of glue or pins to hold doilies in place.

4. Lightly spray paper with paint. Let dry. Remove doilies.

Printing ideas with FOAM INSOLES (WHAT??)

THAT'S RIGHT! HERE'S WHAT YOU NEED TO DO:

SUPPLIES:

SMALL PAINT ROLLER
FOAM INSOLES FOR SHOES
PENCIL OR MARKER
GLUE

1. USE PENCIL OR MARKER TO TRACE DESIGNS ON FOAM INSOLES. CUT 'EM OUT.

2. GLUE DESIGNS ONTO PAINT ROLLER. SPACE 'EM EVENLY AROUND ROLLER & FILL THE WIDTH OF THE ROLLER, TOO.

3. TO PRINT, BRUSH A THIN LAYER OF PAINT IN A TRAY— RUN ROLLER THROUGH PAINT. ROLL ON PAPER!

71

Gifts from the Kitchen

Wish friends and family a Merry Christmas with yummy creations from your country kitchen. Choose from spicy pumpkin-apple pie, tasty sauces and spreads, luscious cheesecake bars, sweet treats and fragrant loaves of just-baked bread. Then dress up your treasures in homespun and raffia...package them in containers that become gifts in themselves. Spread the Christmas spirit by sharing the delights on the following pages with those you hold dear!

Pretty tie-ons...homespun, jute, raffia, buttons and handmade labels...let folks know that your gifts were prepared with generous helpings of tender loving care! Recipes for the yummy sauces and spreads that fill these canning jars begin on page 74, and instructions for the decorated jars are on pages 130-131.

homemade
Apple
Butter

homemade
Apple
Butter

Joy to You...
at Christmas

Vegetable
Relish

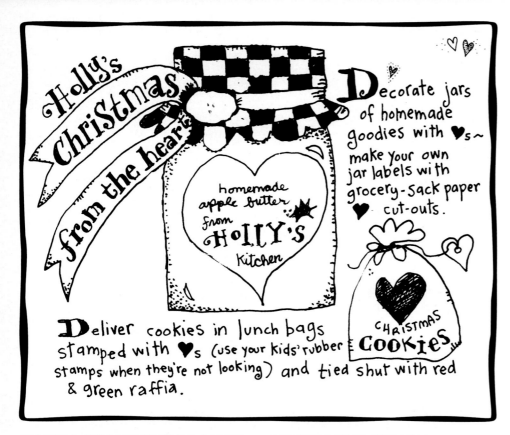

Holly's Christmas from the heart

homemade apple butter from HOLLY'S Kitchen

Decorate jars of homemade goodies with ♥s~ make your own jar labels with grocery-sack paper ♥ cut-outs.

CHRISTMAS COOKIES

Deliver cookies in lunch bags stamped with ♥s (use your kids' rubber stamps when they're not looking) and tied shut with red & green raffia.

SPICY APPLE BUTTER
Try this apple butter on pancakes too!

4 lbs. apples, stemmed and
    quartered
1 c. apple cider
2¹/2 c. sugar
1 t. cinnamon
1 t. cloves
¹/2 t. allspice

Cook the apples and cider in a slow cooker 10 hours or overnight on high. Sift the apples through a food mill and return pulp to the slow cooker. Add the balance of the ingredients and cook one hour longer. You may want to leave lid off slow cooker to cook off some liquid. Ladle into hot, sterilized pint jars, leaving ¹/4-inch headspace. Process in a boiling water canner for 10 minutes.

Michelle Maris
Lincoln, IL

RAISIN-CRANBERRY SAUCE
A delicious glaze for your holiday ham or turkey!

2¹/4 c. golden raisins
2 c. orange juice
1 c. water
¹/4 c. lemon juice
²/3 c. sugar
3 c. fresh or frozen cranberries
1 T. orange zest, finely grated

Combine raisins, orange juice, water, lemon juice and sugar in a 3-quart saucepan. Bring to a boil and stir until sugar dissolves. Reduce heat and simmer for 10 minutes. Add the cranberries and simmer 5 more minutes. Add orange zest and simmer another 5 minutes, until liquid barely covers solid ingredients; cool. Store in fridge for up to one month; freezer for a year. Yield: 4¹/2 cups.

Laura Mastropaolo
Huron, OH

Share flower seeds from your garden with a special friend. Package your gift in decorated half-pint canning jars.

VEGETABLE RELISH
This makes a nice, quick Christmas gift. Everyone enjoys homemade goodies!

6 lg. onions
12 green peppers
1 med. head cabbage
6 sweet red peppers
10 green tomatoes
¹/2 c. granulated pickling salt
6 c. sugar
2 T. mustard seed
1 T. celery seed
1¹/2 t. turmeric
4 c. cider vinegar
2 c. water

Wash onions, peppers, cabbage and tomatoes. Grind vegetables, using a coarse blade. Sprinkle with pickling salt and let stand overnight. Rinse and drain. Combine sugar, mustard seed, celery seed, turmeric, cider vinegar and water. Pour over vegetables. Bring to a boil, and let boil gently for 5 minutes. Fill jars with relish. Store in refrigerator. Makes approximately 6 to 7 quarts.

Kim Burns
Ashley, OH

MARY ELIZABETH'S STRAWBERRY JAM
Just wrap up a jar of this yummy jam in a piece of fine white netting and tie it with a pink gingham bow!

3 c. frozen sweetened
    strawberries
3 c. sugar
2 T. lemon juice
1 pkg. powdered pectin
1 c. water

Toss frozen strawberries with sugar and let thaw to dissolve sugar. Add lemon juice. In a saucepan, combine pectin and water. Stirring constantly, bring mixture to a boil. Boil one minute. Remove from heat and stir in berries. Make sure sugar is completely dissolved, about 2 minutes. Pour into freezer containers and cover. Let jam stand at room temperature until mixture has jelled, about 24 hours. Store in freezer if jam is to be kept longer than 6 weeks, otherwise, store in refrigerator.

Easy to make, yummy to eat!

LEMON CURD

Yummy on pound cake!

1 c. sugar
6 T. butter
3 to 4 t. lemon zest, finely
    chopped
6 T. lemon juice
3 eggs, beaten

In the top of a double boiler, combine sugar, butter, zest and lemon juice. Over simmering, not boiling, water, stir mixture until butter has melted and sugar is dissolved. Stirring constantly, spoon a little of the hot butter mixture into beaten eggs. Pour egg mixture into hot butter mixture, stirring constantly to blend. Cook over simmering water until it has thickened, about 20 minutes. Remove lemon curd from heat, cool and refrigerate. Will keep in refrigerator one to 2 weeks.

For an extra special delivery, package holiday treats in our Santa jars, filled here with purchased cinnamon and butterscotch candies. Instructions for the containers are on pages 131-132.

Sweet Noel

RASPBERRY CHEESECAKE BARS

This recipe is a keeper!

1¼ c. all-purpose flour
½ c. brown sugar, packed
½ c. almonds, finely chopped
½ c. shortening
2 8-oz. pkgs. cream cheese, softened
⅔ c. sugar
2 eggs
½ t. almond extract
1 c. seedless raspberry preserves or jam
½ c. coconut
½ c. almonds, sliced

In a mixing bowl, combine flour, brown sugar and almonds. Cut in shortening until mixture resembles fine crumbs. Set aside ½ cup of crumb mixture for topping. To make crust, press remaining crumb mixture into bottom of 13"x9" baking pan. Bake in a 350 degree oven for 12 to 15 minutes or until edges are golden. In another mixing bowl, beat cream cheese, sugar, eggs and almond extract until smooth. Spread over hot crust and return to oven for 15 minutes. Spread preserves over cheese mixture, set aside. In a small bowl, combine reserved crumb mixture, coconut and sliced almonds; sprinkle over preserves. Return to oven and bake 15 minutes longer. Cool in pan on a wire rack. Chill for 3 hours before cutting into bars, store in refrigerator.
Makes 32 bars.

Pat Habiger
Spearville, KS

For cute-as-a-button gifts from the kitchen, package your goodies in a delightful assortment of bags, baskets and other containers.

To spread the holiday spirit, line a pretty basket with a homespun napkin and fill with our Raspberry Cheesecake Bars. Finish with a raffia bow and a Christmasy tag.

Wish a dear friend or relative a sweet Noel with delicious foods wrapped in a handmade bread cloth. Instructions for the bread cloth are on page 132.

OATMEAL COUNTRY HERMITS

Always a family favorite!

2 c. quick or old-fashioned oats, uncooked
1¹/2 c. sifted all-purpose flour
1 c. butter, melted
1 c. brown sugar, packed
³/4 c. raisins
¹/2 c. nuts, chopped
1 egg
¹/4 c. milk
1 t. cinnamon
1 t. vanilla extract
³/4 t. salt
¹/2 t. baking soda
¹/4 t. nutmeg

Preheat oven to 350 degrees. In a large bowl combine all ingredients; mix well. Drop batter by rounded teaspoons onto a foil-lined cookie sheet. Bake 8 to 10 minutes or until lightly browned. Cool for one minute on cookie sheet; remove to wire cooling rack. Store in tightly covered container. Makes 3¹/2 delicious dozen.

Judy Hand
Centre Hall, PA

GINGERBREAD MEN

A great cookie jar cookie.

1 c. butter
1 c. sugar
¹/2 c. dark corn syrup
1 t. cinnamon
1 t. nutmeg
1 t. cloves
1 t. ginger
2 eggs, well beaten
1 t. vinegar
5 c. all-purpose flour
1 t. baking soda

Cream butter with sugar. Add corn syrup and spices. Heat in a saucepan, on stove, stirring constantly. Bring to a boil. Remove from heat and allow to cool. When lukewarm, stir in eggs and vinegar. Sift together flour and baking soda. Stir into wet mixture to form a smooth dough. Chill for several hours or overnight. Roll out; cut with your favorite cookie cutter. Bake at 350 degrees for 8 to 10 minutes.

Michele Dafgek
Ashburn , VA

One of my fondest childhood memories is of our family Christmas tree. Everything on the tree was edible...candy, walnuts, popcorn balls and the best part, gingerbread men. Before baking the gingerbread men, my mother would take a needle and string and thread the string through the cookie. After the cookies baked, we would knot the string and decorate the cookie with icing and it was all ready to hang on the tree. The whole family would decorate the cookies. There would be a cookie decorated for all family members. Couples could be made by baking the cookies with hands touching so they looked like they were holding hands on the tree. As guests left, my mother would give them cookies to take home, often personalized.

Michele Dafgek
Ashburn, VA

11

Just for You

MOM'S HOT CHOCOLATE

3½ c. powdered sugar
3¼ c. instant nonfat dry milk
2 c. instant chocolate drink powder
½ c. malted milk powder, chocolate flavor
¼ c. cocoa powder
¾ c. nondairy creamer (regular or flavored)

Mix all ingredients together thoroughly and store in an airtight container. Include these directions with mix: Place ⅓ cup of mix in an 8 or 10-ounce mug. Pour ¾ cup of hot water over mix and stir to dissolve. For a richer cup of cocoa, try using warm milk in place of water.

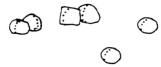

Chilly winter days call for generous helpings of steaming hot chocolate. A thoughtful present, this delicious, quick-to-mix drink makes a heartwarming gift when presented with a snowman mug mat. Instructions for the homespun gift bag are on page 132.

MUG MAT

Brighten a table or gift bag full of goodies this holiday season by adding one of our cheerful mug mats. Begin by tracing the snowman design, page 157, onto tracing paper. Use transfer paper to transfer the design onto 24-count linen. Using 2 strands of 3-ply needlepoint yarn, work *French Knots*, page 135, for eyes and buttons...then use one strand of yarn to work French Knots over the rest of the design. Cut out the design ½-inch outside the border; press excess linen to the wrong side of the mat. Using one strand of yarn, whipstitch around the edge of the mat. For the backing, trace around the mat on felt and cut out just inside the drawn line. Use fabric glue to glue the felt piece to the back of the mat.

...and don't forget the marshmallows!

*B*e an elf...leave a present on someone's doorstep!

— MINI — Jingle Bell Wreaths

WHEN THIS JINGLES, THINK OF ME!

...sweet little souvenirs of the season for your friends!

★ THIN FLORIST WIRE ON SPOOL
★ JINGLE BELLS
★ RED RIBBON
★ WIRE CUTTERS OR OLD SCISSORS
★ PRETTY PAPER TAGS (OPTIONAL)

1. Cut wire into desired length. Make a loop at one end.
2. Thread bells onto wire. Form into wreath shape. Twist wire ends together to secure. Clip off excess wire.
3. Tie a gift tag on with ribbon if you like.

"RUNNING BACK" POPCORN 'N PEANUTS

You'll go "running back" for more!

1/2 c. honey
1/4 c. butter
6 c. popped popcorn
1 c. salted peanuts

Heat honey and butter until blended. Mix popcorn and peanuts in a large bowl, and stir in honey butter mixture. Spread mixture into 2 large pans. Bake for 10 minutes at 350 degrees.

Give your favorite snacker a giant tin filled with peanuts, pretzels, chips or party mix. Decorate the outside of a large coffee can with acrylic paint in fun winter designs...snowmen, trees, stars or angels. An irresistible treat!

Jingle all the way to a friend's house as you deliver this sweet snack. It's easy to make a handsome package for a yummy treat like "Running Back" Popcorn 'n Peanuts...simply attach one of our jingle bell wreaths and a hand-lettered tag to a gift bag!

"OK! ALLRIGHT ALREADY! I'LL SHARE! I'LL SHARE!"
— Kate —

SUNSET ORCHARD SPICED TEA MIX

Warm and spicy!
Enjoy this Christmas morning!

1 c. sugar
1/3 c. dry orange drink mix
2/3 c. dry instant tea
2 envelopes (.65 or .72 oz. each)
   instant spiced cider mix

Combine sugar, drink mix and tea together. Blend in cider mix. Place in an airtight container. For each 7 ounces of hot water used, add 3 1/2 teaspoons of mix; let steep 2 minutes.

Leekay Bennett
Delaware, OH

APPLE-CHEDDAR TRIPLE LOAVES

Apples and cheddar cheese go together...it's as simple as that!

3 c. all-purpose flour
1/2 c. sugar
2 T. baking powder
3/4 t. salt
1 egg, beaten
1 egg yolk, beaten
1 1/2 c. milk
1/2 c. vegetable oil
3/4 c. apples, diced
3/4 c. Cheddar cheese, shredded

Combine flour, sugar, baking powder and salt in a large mixing bowl. Combine the whole egg, egg yolk, milk and oil in a medium bowl; add to flour mixture and stir just until moistened. Gently fold in the apples and cheese. Divide batter among three greased 7 1/2"x3 1/2" loaf pans. Bake at 350 degrees about 35 minutes or until inserted toothpick comes out clean. Cool 10 minutes and remove from pans. When completely cool, wrap in plastic wrap and store in refrigerator.

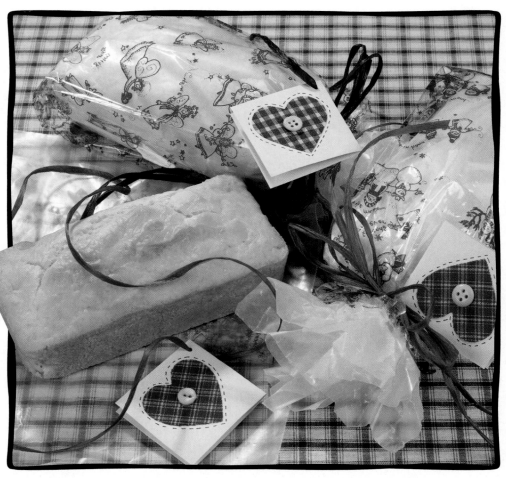

Friends and relatives will love this unbeatable combination! For an appealing touch, package Apple-Cheddar Loaves in cellophane bags with colorful bows and handmade tags. To make the tags, fuse fabric shapes to card stock; add drawn-on "stitches" and a glued button.

SPICED CIDER MIX

Here's a yummy spiced cider mix to warm you up! Combine and store in an airtight container.

3/4 c. brown sugar, packed
2 t. cinnamon
1 t. cloves
1/2 t. orange zest, grated
1 t. allspice
1/2 t. nutmeg (if desired)

To make cider: Combine 1/4 cup mix, one cup apple juice and 1/4 cup water. Bring to a boil over medium heat. Reduce heat and simmer for 5 minutes. Yield: one serving. (Can also be made using red wine instead of apple juice).

Michelle Golz
Freeport, IL

PANCAKE & WAFFLE MIX

Great to give along with the recipe and a pitcher of delicious maple syrup!

Basic Mix:
6 c. all-purpose flour
6 T. baking powder
6 T. sugar
2 c. instant nonfat dry milk
1 T. salt

To Make Batter:
1 1/2 c. basic mix
1 c. water
1 egg, beaten
2 T. vegetable oil

Beat ingredients with a fork. Fry in a tiny bit of oil in a skillet. For extra nutrients, add 2 tablespoons raw wheat germ to batter.

Susan Kirschenheiter
Lexington, OH

Surprise someone at mealtime with a warm loaf of bread and a crock of whipped butter!

BAVARIAN MINT COFFEE MIX
Relax and enjoy!

1/3 c. nondairy creamer
1/3 c. sugar
1/3 c. instant coffee crystals
2 T. cocoa powder
5 hard peppermint candies,
   crushed

Combine all together. Store in an airtight container. Use 2 to 2 1/2 teaspoons per cup of boiling water.

Cheryl Ewer
Bismarck, ND

BROWNIE MIX
This makes several gifts.

4 c. all-purpose flour
6 c. sugar
3 c. cocoa powder
4 t. baking powder
3 t. salt
2 c. vegetable shortening

Combine and mix well: flour, sugar, cocoa, baking powder and salt. Using pastry blender, thoroughly cut in vegetable shortening. Store in airtight container in cool dry place (can freeze, but bring to room temperature before making).
Yield: 8 batches

To use mix:
2 c. mix
2 eggs
1 t. vanilla extract
1/2 c. chopped nuts (if desired)

Combine all ingredients; stir until moist. Spread in lightly greased 8" square pan. Bake in preheated 350 degree oven for 20 to 25 minutes, or until set in the center. Cut into 2" squares. Yield: 16 brownies.

Variations: Add one cup of chocolate chips, butterscotch chips, hot fudge sauce, caramel ice cream topping or chopped maraschino cherries.

Michelle Golz
Freeport, IL

81

For pleasing presents, deliver tasty treats like Bavarian Mint Coffee Mix, Vanilla Coffee and Brownie Mix in cute homespun bags adorned with seasonal motifs.

Instructions for the bags are on page 133.

Handpaint a design on a bag, fold over to close ... and sew a button on to keep it shut!

*B*e prepared ahead of time with gifts for friends who drop by during the holidays...cups filled with gourmet coffees, teas, cocoas and gingerbread men, or cookie cutters with your favorite Christmas cookie recipe attached.

VANILLA COFFEE
Keep on hand for guests.

1 1/2 c. nondairy creamer
1 c. dry hot chocolate mix
1/2 t. nutmeg
1 t. cinnamon
1 1/2 c. sugar
1/2 c. instant coffee crystals
2 T. vanilla powder

Mix all ingredients together and place in cellophane bags. When ready to use, put 2 to 4 tablespoons in a mug of boiling water and enjoy. If you wish to use sugar substitute instead of sugar, omit sugar from ingredients and add sugar substitute (to taste) in mug.

Judy Borecky
Escondido, CA

APRICOT-PECAN NUT BREAD
Serve with Orange Blossom Butter.

2½ c. all-purpose flour
1¼ c. sugar
3½ t. baking powder
2 T. orange zest, grated
1 t. lemon zest, grated
1 t. salt
3 T. vegetable oil
½ c. milk
1 egg
¾ c. orange juice
1½ c. pecans, chopped
2 c. dried apricots, chopped

Measure all ingredients into large mixing bowl. Mix for about 2 minutes by hand or one minute with electric mixer. Pour into a greased and floured 9"x5" loaf pan. Bake for one hour at 350 degrees. Test with toothpick in center to make sure it's done. Let cool. Slice and serve.

Jane Gossett
Harrison, ID

ORANGE BLOSSOM BUTTER
Mighty good spread!

½ c. butter, softened
2 T. orange juice
1 t. orange zest, finely grated
3 T. powdered sugar

In a small bowl, beat ingredients together until light and fluffy.

DATE-PECAN LOAF
Try a slice with a green salad, or have with hot coffee or tea.

Loaf:
1 c. sugar
½ c. applesauce
⅓ c. vegetable oil
2 eggs
3 t. milk
½ c. dates, chopped fine
2 c. all-purpose flour, sifted
1 t. baking soda
½ t. baking powder
¼ t. salt
¼ t. nutmeg
¾ c. pecans, chopped

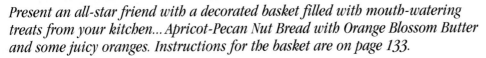

Present an all-star friend with a decorated basket filled with mouth-watering treats from your kitchen... Apricot-Pecan Nut Bread with Orange Blossom Butter and some juicy oranges. Instructions for the basket are on page 133.

Instead of stockings, give everyone a holiday basket!

Topping:

1/4 c. brown sugar, packed
1/4 t. cinnamon
1/4 c. pecans, chopped

Combine sugar, applesauce, oil, eggs and milk. Stir in dates. In separate bowl, sift together flour, baking soda, baking powder, salt and nutmeg. Add to wet mixture and beat until well combined. Stir in pecans. Pour batter into greased loaf pan. Make topping by combining brown sugar, cinnamon and pecans and sprinkle evenly over batter. Bake at 350 degrees for one hour. Cover loosely with foil after first 30 minutes of baking. Test with toothpick. Remove from pan and allow to cool.

HERBAL SPICED CIDER MIX

*Flavorful herbs give this
mix a special taste.*

1/4 t. cardamom seeds
1 t. whole allspice
1 t. whole cloves
1 stick cinnamon
1/2 T. dried lemon balm, chopped
3 T. dried orange mint, chopped
1 t. dried lemon verbena, chopped
2 t. dried lemon basil, chopped

Mix all together in a bowl. Place in a plastic bag and tie shut with a ribbon. Make a sticker with the directions for how to prepare, and attach to bag; or put directions on a little card, punch a hole in the corner of the card and tie on with the ribbon.

DIRECTIONS: Add about 3 tablespoons mix to one quart apple cider, cranberry juice or red wine. Simmer for 10 minutes. Remove from heat, cover and steep 20 to 30 minutes. Strain and serve.

*Jan Jacobson
Madison, WI*

Skip traditional gift wrap and make the container a part of the gift! Baskets, Shaker boxes, crocks, jars and tins make wonderful gifts in addition to what's tucked inside!

A holiday host or hostess will get double enjoyment out of this festive gift! Homemade Cheese Straws and a flavorful bottled drink can be served on the spot, with the cider mix saved for later! For an impressive presentation, package the edibles in a handsome container trimmed with greenery and fabric bows.

CHEESE STRAWS

Everyone enjoys this cheesy treat.

2 c. Cheddar cheese, grated
1/2 c. butter, softened
1/8 t. hot pepper sauce or sprinkle
   of red pepper
yolk of 1 egg
1 1/2 c. all-purpose flour
1/4 t. salt

Mix like pie crust. Roll out, cut in narrow strips and bake at 350 degrees for 10 to 15 minutes.

*Jeanne Calkins
Midland, MI*

SHORT and SWEET IDEAS FOR GIFTS to GO

Italian Soup

... a gift to warm the heart and tummy!

ITALIAN TORTELLINI SOUP
You'll get requests for this recipe!

1 lb. mild Italian sausage, casing removed
1 c. onion, chopped
2 lg. cloves garlic, chopped
6 c. beef stock
16-oz. can tomatoes, drained and chopped
8-oz. can tomato sauce
1 lg. zucchini, sliced
1 lg. carrot, sliced
1 med. green pepper, diced
½ c. dry red wine
1 t. dried basil leaves
2 t. oregano
8 oz. cheese tortellini
Parmesan cheese

Brown sausage and remove from skillet. Drain drippings. Add onion and garlic. Sauté 5 minutes. Combine meat, onion and garlic, beef stock, tomatoes, tomato sauce, zucchini, carrot, green pepper, wine and spices in a large pot. Simmer about 30 minutes or until vegetables are tender. Add tortellini. Cook until tender. Serve with cheese.

Teresa Sullivan
Westerville, OH

Looking for a unique gift idea? Give all the makings for a great Italian dinner! Fill a stockpot with pasta, sauces, garlic, herbs and wooden spoons.

Delight a friend or family member during the holidays by delivering dinner to their door. Topped with homespun and a buttoned-up jute bow, a canning jar of hearty Italian Tortellini Soup makes an appetizing gift, especially when presented in a pottery crock.

PUMPKIN DUTCH APPLE PIE

Two favorite flavors in one wonderful pie.

Apple Layer:
2 med. Granny Smith apples,
    peeled, cored and thinly sliced
1/4 c. sugar
2 t. all-purpose flour
1 t. lemon juice
1/4 t. cinnamon
1 9" deep-dish pie shell, unbaked

Pumpkin Layer:
2 eggs, lightly beaten
1 1/2 c. solid-pack pumpkin
1 c. undiluted evaporated milk
1/2 c. sugar
2 T. butter, melted
3/4 t. cinnamon
1/8 t. nutmeg
1/4 t. salt

Crumble Topping:
1/2 c. all-purpose flour
5 T. sugar
3 T. butter, softened
1/3 c. walnuts, chopped

For apple layer, toss apples with sugar, flour, lemon juice and cinnamon. Place in pie shell.

For pumpkin layer, combine eggs, pumpkin, evaporated milk, sugar, butter, cinnamon, nutmeg and salt. Pour over apple layer. Bake in a preheated oven at 375 degrees for 30 minutes. While pie is baking, mix together ingredients for crumble topping. Remove pie from oven and sprinkle with topping. Return to oven and bake for an additional 20 minutes or until custard is set. Cool.

Made in layers, Pumpkin Dutch Apple Pie combines the delicious appeal of two traditional favorites. Instructions for the charming gift tag are on page 133.

"What calls back the past, like the rich pumpkin pie?"

— John Greenleaf Whittier

Mary Murray
Gooseberry Patch

85

Festive Foods & Glorious Feasts

As Kate, Holly & Mary Elizabeth all know, it's just not Christmas without an abundance of good food and good friends! No one can resist a treat from the cookie jar or a yummy dessert. Serve up a little fun with an open house, invite the neighbors for coffee, plan a holiday brunch or a sit-down dinner...there's always room for more helpings from the Christmas groaning board!

For an impressive Christmas-Day dinner, serve a standing Pork Crown Roast with Fruit Glaze...it's easier to prepare than you might think! Check out the recipe on page 114.

Yuletide SWEETS

Make your Christmas memorable with our country kitchen sweets...a festive collection of traditional holiday fare and fun foods like triple delight fudge cake!

Sugar Crispies

Spread melted chocolate generously on one side of a sugar cookie. Stick another cookie on top to make a sandwich. You can melt the chocolate squares or chips in the microwave or a double boiler. Put your sandwich cookies in the fridge to set for a few minutes...then decorate.

SUGAR CRISPIES
An easy cookie to make with the kids!

1 c. shortening
2 c. sugar
2 eggs
1 c. oil
1/2 t. salt
1 t. vanilla extract
5 c. all-purpose flour
2 t. baking soda
2 t. cream of tartar
sugar for coating
gumdrops

Cream together shortening, sugar, eggs, oil, salt and vanilla. Sift all dry ingredients and add to creamed mixture. Roll into one-inch balls and roll in sugar. Press one gumdrop in center of each cookie. Bake at 350 degrees for 10 minutes. Yield: 8 dozen.

Peggy Peters
Chittenango, NY

NUTMEG LOGS
You can shape these into rainbows and dip in multicolored sprinkles.

1 c. butter or margarine, softened
2 t. vanilla extract
1 t. almond extract
3/4 c. sugar
1 egg
3 c. all-purpose flour
1 1/2 t. nutmeg
1/4 t. salt
6 oz. chocolate chips, melted
chocolate jimmies or sprinkles

Cream butter with flavorings. Gradually beat in sugar, then blend in egg. Mix together flour, nutmeg and salt. Add to butter mixture and mix well. Divide into 14 equal pieces. On a sugared board, shape each piece into a roll 12 inches long and 1/2 inch in diameter. Cut into 2-inch lengths and put on greased cookie sheets. Bake in a preheated 350 degree oven for 12 minutes. When cool, dip both ends in melted chocolate chips, then in jimmies. Makes about 7 dozen.

Donna Kincaid
Clarksboro, NJ

Begin stocking your pantry in the fall with those things you'll need for baking around the holidays...chocolate chips, vanilla, dried and candied fruits, sugar, flour, pecans and extras like gumdrops and chocolate sprinkles.

Homemade shortbread cookies tied with colorful ribbon look beautiful hanging in your windowpanes.

SPICY GINGER COOKIES
These cookies smell so good baking!

1 c. butter or margarine, softened
1 c. brown sugar, packed
1/4 c. molasses
1 egg
2 1/4 c. all-purpose flour
2 t. baking soda
1/4 t. salt
1 t. cinnamon
1 t. ginger
1/2 t. cloves
sugar

Cream together butter or margarine and brown sugar. Stir in molasses and egg until well blended. Combine flour, baking soda, salt, cinnamon, ginger and cloves. Add to molasses mixture. Roll into one-inch balls and roll in sugar. Place on ungreased baking sheet. Bake in 350 degree oven for 10 to 12 minutes. Cool. Serve.

PAY DAY BARS
As satisfying as pay day!

Base:
1 box yellow cake mix
1 egg
2/3 c. butter, softened
2 c. mini marshmallows

Mix all ingredients (except marshmallows) together. Press in a jelly roll pan and bake at 350 degrees for 12 minutes. On top of base, add the marshmallows and bake for 5 more minutes.

Topping:
10-oz. pkg. peanut butter chips
2 T. butter
2/3 c. corn syrup
2 c. crispy rice cereal
2 c. salted peanuts

Melt chips, butter and syrup in a saucepan. Add cereal and peanuts. Pour over the base. Cool; cut into squares.

Gloria & Michele Mosholder

TOFFEE BAR CRUNCH BISCOTTI
Magical! You'll fall under their spell!

6 T. butter, melted
1/3 c. oil
1/2 c. sugar
1/4 c. brown sugar, packed
2 t. vanilla extract
1 t. butterscotch extract
3 eggs, beaten
3 c. all-purpose flour
1 3/4 t. baking powder
1/4 t. salt
1 1/2 c. chocolate-covered toffee bar, chopped
1/2 c. pecans, toasted and coarsely chopped

Cream together butter, oil, sugar and brown sugar in medium bowl. Mix in vanilla and butterscotch extracts. Add eggs. Combine dry ingredients and stir into creamed mixture. Add chopped toffee bar and pecans. Line baking sheet with parchment paper. Dough will be sticky, so lightly flour hands. Form into 2 logs about 8"x3". Bake at 350 degrees for 25 to 30 minutes or until center is set. Cool for 10 to 15 minutes. Slice crosswise into 1/2-inch slices. Return slices, cut side down, to baking sheet. Bake 10 to 12 minutes on one side, then turn over and bake opposite side an additional 5 minutes. Cool on wire racks.

Dip your measuring cup in hot water before measuring butter; it will slip out without sticking.

Holly's CRISPY SHORTBREAD SNACKS
...QUICK & EASY·BUT·ELEGANT·AND·ABSOLUTELY·THE·MOST· DELICIOUS·LITTLE·COOKIE·YOU·EVER·HAD·WITH·A·MUG·OF· MOCHA·IN·YOUR·ENTIRE·LIFE·I·JUST·CAN'T·TELL·YOU·HOW· GOOD·IT·IS·I·GUESS·YOU'LL·HAVE·TO·TRY·IT·YOURSELF!

3/4 c. FLOUR
1/3 c. SUGAR
1/4 c. CORNSTARCH
1/4 t. ANISE SEED, CHOPPED
1/2 c. UNSALTED BUTTER, MELTED & COOLED

COMBINE FLOUR, SUGAR, CORNSTARCH & ANISE SEED IN MEDIUM BOWL. POUR BUTTER OVER DRY MIXTURE ~ STIR WELL. PRESS DOUGH EVENLY INTO 9" PIE PLATE. BAKE 25 TO 30 MINUTES IN 325° OVEN ~ PIERCE WITH FORK IF DOUGH PUFFS UP. REMOVE WHEN GOLDEN BROWN & CUT INTO 8 WEDGES. COOL COMPLETELY ~ DIP INTO MELTED CHOCOLATE, IF DESIRED.

TRIPLE DELIGHT FUDGE CAKE

A CHOCOLATE LOVER'S DREAM!

Cake:
cocoa powder
deep chocolate or fudge cake mix
3.9-oz. pkg. chocolate fudge
    instant pudding mix
1/4 c. oil, only if mix calls for oil
3 to 4 eggs
1/4 c. mayonnaise
water (amount on cake mix)

Grease three 8" round layer pans and dust with cocoa. Combine ingredients in a mixing bowl. Beat for about 2 minutes. Pour into pans. Bake according to package instructions, about 30 minutes, or until toothpick inserted in center comes out clean. Cool in pans 5 minutes, then invert and cool on racks.

Mousse Filling:
3.9-oz. pkg. chocolate fudge
    instant pudding mix
1 to 1 1/4 c. milk
3/4 c. whipped topping
1 t. instant coffee or 2 T. Kahlua

Mix pudding and milk together. Fold in whipped topping and coffee or Kahlua. Chill.

To assemble cake, place one layer on a cake plate and spread a layer of mousse on top. Top with 2nd cake layer. Again, spread with mousse. Top with final cake layer. For a really elegant 6-layer cake, split cake layers and fill with mousse as well. Keep well chilled. About an hour before serving, top cake with glaze.

Glaze:
1 1/2 c. semi-sweet chocolate chips
1 T. light corn syrup
1/4 c. butter

Combine ingredients in a double boiler. Stir until chips are completely melted and glaze is smooth and glossy. Spread over top and let drip down sides of cake. (If it seems too thick, heat and add a little milk, never water.)

*H*ost a holiday dessert party and invite your friends and neighbors. Serve several different desserts with assorted coffees, cocoa and eggnog. A variety of fruit and cheese is nice, too. As a guideline for your dessert party, choose 3 desserts for 8 people, adding another dessert for each additional 8 as your guest list grows.

SPICY PUMPKIN CHEESECAKE

Forget about calories and enjoy!

1 egg yolk
1 extra large graham cracker pie
    crust
2 8-oz. pkgs. cream cheese,
    softened
1/2 to 3/4 c. sugar
2 eggs
15-oz. can pumpkin
1 1/2 t. cinnamon
1/2 t. ginger
1/4 t. cloves
Garnish: whipped topping and
    toasted pecan halves

Beat egg yolk and brush on crust. Bake at 350 degrees for 5 minutes, then set aside. In a large mixing bowl, beat cream cheese, sugar and eggs at medium speed until smooth. Add pumpkin and remaining spices; continue mixing until well blended. Spoon into pie crust and bake at 350 degrees for 40 to 45 minutes or until set. Cool and refrigerate several hours or overnight. Garnish with whipped topping and toasted pecan halves.

Sharon Hall
Gooseberry Patch

PEANUT BUTTER POUND CAKE

Delicious without the frosting, too!

1 c. butter, softened
2 c. sugar
1 c. light brown sugar, packed
1/2 c. creamy peanut butter
5 eggs
1 T. vanilla extract
3 c. cake flour
1/2 t. baking powder
1/2 t. salt
1/4 t. baking soda
1 c. whipping cream or whole milk

Cream butter and sugar until fluffy. Add brown sugar and peanut butter; beat thoroughly. Add eggs, one at a time, beating well after each addition; stir in vanilla. Sift together the dry ingredients and

Make a homemade pastry bag with a resealable plastic sandwich bag. Fill it halfway with the frosting, then close it up. Cut a tiny hole in one corner and you're ready to decorate!

a happy time of year!

add alternately with whipping cream. Pour into a lightly greased and floured very large tube pan. Bake at 325 degrees for one hour or until it tests done. Frost, if desired, with peanut butter frosting.

Frosting:
1/4 c. butter, softened
1/8 t. salt
5 to 6 T. milk
1/3 c. creamy peanut butter
16-oz. box powdered sugar

Combine all ingredients and beat until smooth.

Charolotte Wolfe
Ft. Lauderdale, FL

OLD-FASHIONED FRUITCAKE
What would Christmas be without a fruitcake? You'll like this one.

1 c. butter, softened
2 1/2 c. white sugar
6 eggs
1 bottle (1 oz.) brandy flavoring
4 c. all-purpose flour
1 1/2 t. cinnamon
1 t. nutmeg
1 t. salt
1 1/2 lbs. ready mix candied fruit
1 lb. seedless raisins
3/4 lb. candied pineapple
3/4 lb. whole candied cherries
2 c. pecan halves
Garnish: light corn syrup and
　　　pecan halves

Line angel food pan with foil; set aside. Mix butter, sugar, eggs and flavoring in a large bowl with electric mixer. Sift together next 4 ingredients and mix thoroughly with butter and egg mixture. Work the fruit and nuts into batter with hands. Fill pan 2/3 full with batter. Bake at 275 degrees for 3 hours. One-half hour before cake is done, brush top with light corn syrup. Decorate with pecan halves and finish baking. Cool. Place cake, wrapped in a wine-soaked cloth, in an airtight container. Store in a cool place for several weeks, this blends and mellows the cake.

Cheryl Neff

Triple Delight Fudge Cake

Spicy Pumpkin Cheesecake

FRENCH APPLE CREME PIE

Granny Smith apples add just the right tartness to this delicious pie.

Start with a two-crust unbaked pie shell; roll bottom half and put into pie tin. Roll top half and cut a 2-inch opening in the center. You can use a large, favorite holiday cookie cutter to make this opening, then put aside.

Apple Filling:
3/4 c. sugar
2 T. all-purpose flour
1/2 t. cinnamon
1/2 t. nutmeg
1 T. lemon zest, grated
5 c. Granny Smith apples, peeled
    and sliced
2 T. butter

Combine sugar, flour, cinnamon, nutmeg and lemon zest in a large bowl. Add apples and stir to coat. Turn into pie shell and dot with butter. Top with pie crust that has a 2-inch opening cut into the center. Bake for 10 minutes at 425 degrees and then 30 to 35 minutes at 375 degrees. While your pie is baking, cook the creme sauce.

Creme Sauce:
2 eggs, beaten
1/2 c. sugar
1 T. lemon juice
3-oz. pkg. cream cheese, cut into
    pieces
1/2 c. sour cream

In a saucepan combine eggs, sugar and lemon juice. Cook over medium heat, stirring constantly until thick enough to coat the back of a spoon. Add cream cheese and sour cream. After your pie is baked, spoon through opening in top of crust. Chill before serving.

Carolyn Ritz Lemon
Acworth, GA

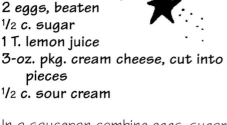

Bake an apple with lots of cinnamon, brown sugar and raisins...tastes just like Christmas!

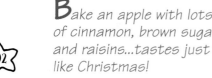

Cream Cheese Brownies, Cranberry Tassies

CREAM CHEESE BROWNIES

I have made these so many times I could bake them with my eyes closed!

8-oz. pkg. cream cheese
2 1/3 c. sugar, divided
3 eggs
1/2 c. butter
3/4 c. water
2/3 c. cocoa powder
2 c. all-purpose flour
1 t. baking soda
1/2 t. salt
1 t. vanilla extract
1/2 c. sour cream
1 c. chocolate chips

Combine cream cheese, 1/3 cup sugar and one egg; set aside. Mix butter, water and cocoa in a saucepan and heat until butter is melted. Mix together flour, remaining sugar, baking soda, salt, vanilla, 2 eggs and sour cream. Beat chocolate into flour mixture. Spread into a greased and floured 17 1/2"x11" pan. Spoon cream cheese mixture over chocolate mixture and marble with a knife. Sprinkle chocolate chips on top. Bake at 375 degrees for 20 to 25 minutes. Makes 32 brownies.

Jean Landolfi
Northford, CT

CRANBERRY TASSIES

Tart and crunchy...a terrific combination!

1/2 c. butter, softened
3-oz. pkg. cream cheese, softened
1 c. all-purpose flour
1 egg
3/4 c. brown sugar, packed
1 T. butter, melted
1 t. orange zest, grated
1/2 c. cranberries, chopped
1/2 c. pecans, chopped

In a mixing bowl, cream butter and cream cheese; stir in flour and blend well. Cover and chill for one hour. In a separate bowl, mix together egg, brown sugar, melted butter and orange zest. Fold in cranberries and pecans. Remove chilled dough from refrigerator and roll into 24 one-inch balls. Place each ball in an ungreased miniature muffin cup; pressing dough along the bottom and up the sides. Spoon cranberry mixture into the center of each cup. Bake at 325 degrees for 30 minutes or until cranberry filling is set. Allow to cool before serving.

ANNIE'S BREAD PUDDING

Bread pudding fills the house with a "welcome home" aroma. It is especially good topped with half-and-half or milk.

¼ c. butter, softened
¾ t. ginger
½ t. cinnamon
¼ t. salt
8 slices bread
½ c. raisins
4 eggs, beaten
¼ c. honey
¼ c. brown sugar, packed
4 c. milk

Cream first 4 ingredients together until fluffy. Spread each bread slice with butter mixture and layer with raisins in 9"x5" loaf pan. Combine eggs, honey, brown sugar and milk in a large mixing bowl and pour over bread. Allow to stand 15 to 20 minutes. Place loaf pan in another baking dish half filled with water. Bake at 325 degrees for one hour or until knife inserted in center comes out clean.

Annie Bateman
Maple Plain, MN

Bake a Christmas pudding, an old English tradition! For luck, add a tiny horseshoe charm; for wealth, a silver coin; for marriage, a silver ring. Whoever gets the charm in his or her dessert has good luck in the coming new year!

Cut baked gingerbread into squares and place a clean stencil on top...sprinkle with powdered sugar and gently remove stencil!

Dear Santa,
All I want for Christmas is a slice of that cake.
(BUT I WANT IT NOW)
♥ love, Kate

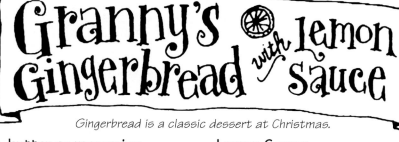

Granny's Gingerbread with Lemon Sauce

Gingerbread is a classic dessert at Christmas.

¼ c. butter or margarine, softened
¼ c. sugar
1 egg
½ c. light molasses
1 c. all-purpose flour
½ t. baking powder
¼ t. baking soda
¼ t. salt
½ t. ginger
½ t. cinnamon
⅛ t. allspice
⅛ t. cloves
6 T. warm water

Preheat oven to 350 degrees. Cream butter and sugar together in a medium-size bowl. Next, add egg and molasses; beat well. Combine flour, baking powder, baking soda and spices together in a small bowl. Alternating with water, gradually add the dry ingredients to the creamed mixture. Pour batter into a greased 8"x8" pan. Bake 35 to 45 minutes or until a toothpick inserted in center comes out clean.

Lemon Sauce:
¾ c. sugar
1½ T. corn starch
1 c. water
½ c. apple cider or juice
5 T. lemon juice
1 T. butter
½ t. lemon zest, finely grated
⅛ t. salt

In a saucepan, combine sugar, corn starch, water and cider. Stir constantly over medium heat; bring to a boil. Reduce heat to low and simmer. Stir until thickened and clear. Remove from stove and stir in lemon juice, butter, zest and salt. Serve warm over gingerbread.

You'll give three cheers for this double delight!

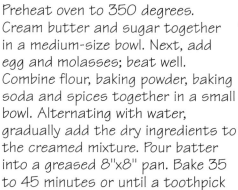

Granny's Gingerbread with Lemon Sauce

CHOCOLATE SNOWBALL TRUFFLES

Your chocolate-craving friends will be delighted!

1/2 c. whipping cream
1/4 c. unsalted butter
1/8 t. salt
8 oz. semi-sweet or bittersweet chocolate, chopped
1 t. vanilla extract
2 T. cocoa powder
2 T. powdered sugar, plus extra for coating

In a saucepan, warm cream, butter and salt over low heat until butter is melted. Stir in chocolate. Cook until chocolate is melted and smooth. Remove from heat and stir in vanilla. Pour mixture into medium bowl, cover with plastic wrap and refrigerate until firm, about 3 hours. In a small bowl, mix together cocoa and 2 tablespoons powdered sugar. Place bowl of chocolate in larger bowl of ice water to keep mixture firm. Using a melon baller or 2 teaspoons dipped in powdered sugar, scoop some chilled chocolate into small balls. Roll ball in cocoa-sugar mixture. You can sprinkle your fingers and palms with powdered sugar and shape the mixture by hand, but you'll need to work quickly to keep the chocolate from melting. After coating each truffle, place them in the refrigerator. Let truffles stand at room temperature for 10 to 15 minutes before serving; do not let them remain at room temperature very long or they will become too soft.

Mary Murray
Gooseberry Patch

Dip pretzel rods in semi-sweet chocolate and then roll them in sprinkled goodies...coconut, crushed nuts, cookie sprinkles or small candies are all terrific!

WHITE CHOCOLATE FUDGE

Try this recipe using almonds or macadamia nuts, too.

2 c. sugar
3/4 c. sour cream
1/2 c. margarine
12 oz. white chocolate, coarsely chopped
7-oz. jar marshmallow cream
3/4 c. walnuts, chopped
3/4 c. dried apricots, chopped

Combine sugar, sour cream and margarine in heavy 2 1/2 to 3-quart saucepan; bring to full rolling boil, stirring constantly. Continue boiling 7 minutes over medium heat or until candy thermometer reaches 234 degrees, stirring constantly to prevent scorching. Remove from heat; stir in chocolate until melted. Add remaining ingredients; beat until well blended. Pour into greased 8 or 9-inch square baking pan. Makes 2 1/2 pounds.

Judy Kelly
St. Charles, MO

BECKY'S CARAMELS

A tradition in my family for the last 25 years.

3 c. light corn syrup
4 c. sugar
1 lb. butter (not margarine)
2 c. whipping cream, divided
1 t. salt
4 c. chopped pecans
2 t. vanilla extract

In a large 6-quart Dutch oven, mix the syrup, sugar, butter and one cup of the cream. Cook over medium to medium-high heat for 15 minutes, then add the other cup of cream and the salt. Cook until 245 degrees or firm ball stage is reached. Before removing from heat, add the pecans and vanilla. Pour into 2 buttered jelly roll pans. When cool, cut into squares. Wrap in wax paper. Makes a very large amount, plenty to share and tuck into gift baskets.

Rebecca Suiter
Checotah, OK

White Chocolate Fudge

GRANDMA WEISER'S ENGLISH TOFFEE

A favorite family recipe.

1 c. butter
1 c. sugar
1 T. light corn syrup
2 T. water
1 c. almonds
6 oz. chocolate chips

Combine all ingredients in a heavy pan except nuts and chocolate chips. Stirring constantly, cook over medium heat until candy thermometer reads 300 degrees or until candy is thick and golden. Spread on buttered cookie sheet, then sprinkle with chocolate chips. Spread chips evenly until melted and top is completely covered. Sprinkle with almond pieces and refrigerate to set. Crack into pieces before serving.

Deb Weiser
Delaware, OH

CRANBERRY SNOW CANDY

Easy to make and tastes great!

16-oz. pkg. white chocolate
   morsels
1½ c. dried cranberries
1½ c. walnuts, chopped

Melt the white chocolate in a double boiler. When melted, add cranberries and walnuts and drop by spoonfuls onto wax paper until set. Makes several dozen.

Juanita Williams
Jacksonville, OR

TALL GLASS CANISTERS FILLED WITH LAYERS OF DIFFERENT CHRISTMAS CANDIES MAKE A COLORFUL CLAIM ON SIDE TABLES.

Grandma Weiser's English Toffee

GLAZED SPICED PECANS

Make lots of these,
because they will go fast.

³/4 c. sugar
1 egg white
2½ t. water
½ t. cinnamon
¼ t. allspice
¼ t. cloves
¼ t. nutmeg
½ t. salt
8 c. pecans

Mix all ingredients in a large bowl. Spread onto a cookie sheet. Bake at 225 degrees for 30 minutes. Cool on wax paper. Pack in airtight containers. Yield: 8 cups.

Terri Burdoff
Fairmont, WV

SURPRISE CHERRY BALLS

You can cut these in half
to serve...they look great.

¼ c. butter, softened
½ c. peanut butter
2 c. powdered sugar
1 T. milk
16-oz. jar maraschino cherries, well
   drained
5 squares semi-sweet chocolate
2 c. walnuts, chopped

Cream butter and peanut butter. Add sugar gradually; blend in milk. Shape one heaping teaspoon of this mixture around each cherry. Melt chocolate over low heat. Dip balls in the chocolate, roll in chopped nuts and refrigerate or freeze to keep firm.

Shirll Kosmal
Delaware, OH

Oooey gooey Yummy

SERVE UP A LITTLE FUN

HOT SPICED WINE PUNCH

This will be a big hit at your next party.

1 qt. apple juice
1 qt. cranberry juice
1 qt. water
2 c. sugar
4 cinnamon sticks
12 whole cloves
zest of 1 lemon, cut in strips
2 qts. rosé wine
½ c. lemon juice

Combine apple and cranberry juices, water, sugar, cinnamon sticks, cloves and lemon zest in a pan. Bring to a boil. Stir until sugar dissolves. Simmer uncovered for 15 minutes. Add wine and lemon juice. Heat, but do not boil. Serve in punch bowl. Garnish with lemon slices. Serves 40. (Be sure punch bowl is capable of holding hot punch.)

Barbara Heck
Bogota, NJ

OLD-FASHIONED EGGNOG

When was the last time you had real eggnog?

6 eggs
1 c. sugar
½ t. salt
1 qt. light cream
1 c. golden rum
nutmeg

Beat eggs until light and foamy. Add sugar and salt, beating until thick. Combine egg mixture and 2 cups light cream in a large saucepan. Stirring constantly, cook over low heat until mixture coats the back of a metal spoon and reaches 160 degrees on a candy thermometer. Remove from heat. Stir in rum and remaining light cream. Chill several hours. Sprinkle with nutmeg just before serving.

Encourage coffee lovers to add a festive touch to their favorite flavor. Place bowls of cinnamon sticks, orange or lemon zest out for guests to add to their individual cups.

Hot Spiced Wine Punch

96

Enjoy!

WHITE HOT CHOCOLATE

Serve in thick mugs with whipped cream, a dash of cinnamon or cocoa powder and a candy cane.

3 c. half-and-half, divided
2/3 c. vanilla chips
3-inch cinnamon stick
1/8 t. nutmeg
1 t. vanilla extract
1/4 t. almond extract
ground cinnamon

In a saucepan, combine 1/4 cup of the half-and-half, vanilla chips, cinnamon stick and nutmeg. Whisk over low heat until vanilla chips are melted. Remove cinnamon stick. Add remaining half-and-half. Whisk until heated throughout. Remove from heat and add vanilla and almond extracts. Makes 4 or 5 servings.

Jeanine English
Wylie, TX

RUSSIAN TEA

Russian Tea brings back such wonderful Christmastime memories of cold winter evenings at my grandparents' home.

16 c. water
2 c. sugar
1 t. whole cloves
3 family size teabags
46-oz. can pineapple juice
12-oz. can frozen orange juice
    concentrate
juice of 3 lemons

Boil 8 cups of water, sugar and cloves for 5 minutes. Boil remaining 8 cups of water with teabags. Remove cloves and teabags and combine liquids. Add juices and serve warm.

Suzanne Wyatt
Snellville, GA

White Hot Chocolate, Toffee Bar Crunch Biscotti (recipe on page 89)

for a perfect cup...

Use your best teacups and saucers for serving your holiday tea and cider.

Prepare for a winter's snowstorm...stock your pantry with cocoa and mini marshmallows, and keep some whipped cream and chocolate shavings on hand for a yummy cup of hot chocolate!

Celebrate the beginning of this joyful day by feasting on tasty early morning fare...from casseroles or a fruit compote to coffee cakes and scones.

BRUNCH BAKED EGGS

Accompanying the eggs could be a variety of quick and yeast breads and fresh fruit.

6 c. (24 oz.) Monterey Jack cheese, shredded and divided
12 oz. fresh mushrooms, sliced
1/2 med. onion, chopped
1/4 c. sweet red pepper, thinly sliced
1/4 c. margarine or butter, melted
8 oz. cooked ham, cut into julienne strips
8 eggs, beaten
1 3/4 c. milk
1/2 c. all-purpose flour
2 T. fresh chives, basil, tarragon, thyme or oregano, snipped
1 T. fresh parsley, snipped

Brunch Baked Eggs, Hot Fruit Compote

Sprinkle 3 cups cheese in the bottom of a 13"x9" baking dish. In a saucepan, cook the mushrooms, onion and red pepper in the margarine until vegetables are tender but not brown. Drain well. Place vegetables over the cheese. Arrange ham strips over vegetables. Sprinkle remaining 3 cups cheese over ham. Cover and chill in refrigerator overnight. To serve, combine eggs, milk, flour, chives and parsley. Pour over cheese layer. Bake at 350 degrees about 45 minutes. Let stand 10 minutes. Serves 12.

Leona Keeley
White Plains, NY

Place your onions in the freezer for 5 minutes before slicing them; no more tears!

HASH BROWN POTATO CASSEROLE

Always a hit with the breakfast crowd.

1/2 c. butter
10 3/4-oz. can cream of mushroom soup
1 pt. sour cream
1/4 c. onion, chopped
1/2 c. Cheddar cheese, shredded (or pasteurized processed cheese spread)
2 lbs. hash brown potatoes

Heat butter with soup. Blend in the rest of the ingredients. Stir in thawed potatoes. Place in a 2 1/2-quart buttered casserole. Bake at 350 degrees for 45 minutes to one hour. Makes 10 to 12 servings.

Linda Tittle
Sanford, FL

HOT FRUIT COMPOTE

You can make this a day ahead... just bake before guests arrive.

15 1/4-oz. can pear halves, cut
15 1/4-oz. can peach halves, cut
15 1/4-oz. can pineapple tidbits
11-oz. can mandarin oranges
3/4 c. brown sugar, packed
1/2 c. margarine, melted
1 1/2 T. corn starch
1 t. curry powder

Drain juice from all fruit. Blend fruit together and place in an 11"x7" baking dish. Combine remaining ingredients in a saucepan and heat, but not to boiling. Pour over fruit. Bake for one hour at 325 degrees.

Sherry Ward
Greenville, OH

GINGERBREAD COFFEE CAKE

*Ten times better than any
store-bought coffee cake!*

1 c. water
1 c. molasses
1 t. baking soda
1 c. brown sugar, packed
1/2 c. butter, softened
2 eggs, beaten
2 c. all-purpose flour
1 T. baking powder
1 t. cinnamon
1/4 t. ginger
1/4 t. cloves

Preheat oven to 350 degrees.
Grease a 13"x9" baking pan. Bring
water and molasses to a boil. Stir
in baking soda. Let cool. Beat sugar,
butter and eggs in a bowl. In
another bowl, combine flour, baking
powder, cinnamon, ginger and cloves.
Beat flour alternately with
molasses, half at a time, into
butter mixture until well mixed. Pour
into the prepared pan.

Topping:
1/3 c. all-purpose flour
1/3 c. sugar
1/2 t. cinnamon
1/2 t. ginger
1/2 c. walnuts, chopped
3 T. butter

Combine flour, sugar, cinnamon,
ginger and walnuts in a bowl. Cut in
butter with a pastry blender until
mixture is coarsely crumbled.
Sprinkle over gingerbread. Bake at
350 degrees for 40 minutes.

Glaze:
1 c. powdered sugar
1 1/2 T. milk
1/2 t. vanilla extract

Whisk sugar, milk and vanilla in
a small bowl until soft enough
to drip from a spoon. If needed,
add more milk. Drizzle over top
of lukewarm cake.

*Jeanine English
Wylie, TX*

Gingerbread Coffee Cake, Holly's Home for Christmas Cider

CRANBERRY BUTTERMILK MUFFINS

*You can make these muffins with
1/4 cup of applesauce and half the oil.*

1 lg. egg
1 c. buttermilk
1/3 c. vegetable oil
1 c. flour (white or whole wheat)
1 1/2 t. baking powder
1/2 t. baking soda
1/2 t. salt
1 c. quick oats
1/2 c. brown sugar, packed
1/2 c. nuts, chopped
1/2 c. dried sweetened cranberries,
    chopped

Beat egg, buttermilk and oil with
whisk. Add remaining ingredients
and stir just until blended. Spoon
into 12 muffin tins prepared with
non-stick spray. Bake at 350
degrees for about 25 minutes,
testing with a toothpick.

*Judy Borecky
Escondido, CA*

Holly's HOME FOR CHRISTMAS Cider

... a warm welcome for your
guests, this cider will scent
your entire house!

- 2 QTS. APPLE JUICE OR CIDER
- 1 QT. CRANBERRY JUICE
- 2 C. ORANGE JUICE
- 1 t. WHOLE CLOVES
- 1 t. WHOLE ALLSPICE
- 1/4 C. SUGAR
- ORANGE SLICES, 1/2" THICK
- CINNAMON STICKS, BROKEN UP

combine all ingredients in
large pan on stove or in
crockpot on low heat. simmer
til blended. Garnish with clove-
studded orange slices & serve
in mugs with cinnamon sticks.

bite-size Sticky buns

Kids love these... they're GOOEY!

5 T. Butter, melted
2 T. Light corn syrup
1/3 c. Brown sugar
1/2 c. Pecans, finely chopped
12 pieces frozen roll dough, thawed

♥

Grease 24 miniature muffin cups. Set aside. Combine butter, corn syrup, sugar & nuts. Spoon mixture into the bottom of muffin cups. Cut each dinner roll in half. Place cut side down on pecan mixture in muffin cup. Cover and let rise in a warm place 'til rolls double in size. Bake at 350° for 15-20 minutes. Remove from oven, cool 1 minute then invert pan on cooling rack or wax-paper.

Bite-Size Sticky Buns

BREAKFAST CHEESECAKE
Tastes like cheese Danish and is so easy to make!

2 8-oz. cans crescent roll dough
2 8-oz. pkgs. cream cheese
1 1/2 c. sugar, divided
1 lg. egg, separated
1 t. vanilla extract
1/2 c. nuts, chopped

Spread one can crescent roll dough in a 13"x9" pan, pressing the perforations together to seal. Combine the cream cheese, one cup of sugar, egg yolk and vanilla and spread on top of the rolls. Lay second can of dough on top of cheese mixture. Beat egg white and brush on top. Mix remaining sugar and nuts together and sprinkle on top. Bake at 350 degrees for 30 minutes.

Barbara Bargdill
Gooseberry Patch

BUTTERY SCONES
Serve warm with butter, honey, jam and, of course, your favorite tea!

1 c. buttermilk (skim is fine)
1 egg
2 to 3 T. sugar
3 1/2 c. unbleached white flour
2 t. baking powder
1 t. baking soda
1/2 t. salt
1/2 c. butter, melted
1/2 c. raisins

With electric mixer, beat buttermilk, egg and sugar together. Sift 3 cups of flour with baking powder, soda and salt. Add 2/3 of the flour mixture to the buttermilk mixture and stir well. Gradually add melted butter, stirring well; add remaining flour mixture. Add raisins and a bit more flour if needed. Knead dough on a floured board for 2 to 3 minutes. Cut dough into 3 parts. Form each into a circle and cut into 4 equal quarters. Butter a cookie sheet. Bake at 400 degrees for 20 to 25 minutes, or until golden brown on top.

Mary Miner

Plump up your raisins by covering them with very warm water and allowing them to sit for 15 minutes. Drain, then let the raisins stand for 4 hours before using.

EGGNOG FRUIT SALAD

Can be made the night before.

1 c. chilled eggnog
1 envelope dry whipped topping mix
1/4 t. nutmeg, freshly grated
16-oz. can sliced peaches, drained
15 1/4-oz. can pineapple tidbits, drained
1 med. apple, chopped
1/4 c. maraschino cherries, drained and halved
1/2 c. fresh or frozen blueberries
1/2 c. walnuts, chopped

In a small bowl, combine eggnog, topping mix and nutmeg. Beat at high speed with electric mixer, until soft peaks form (about 5 minutes). Combine fruits and nuts. Fold into eggnog mixture. Cover and chill in refrigerator for several hours or overnight. Stir gently before serving. Yield: 6 to 8 servings.

Deborah Hilton

Use your kitchen shears to cut canned tomatoes while they're still in the can.

ARTICHOKE & TOMATO CASSEROLE

My mother has prepared this casserole for all important family events ever since I can remember.

2 c. plain bread crumbs
1/2 c. olive oil
3/4 c. Romano cheese, grated
garlic powder to taste
salt and pepper to taste
3 16-oz. pkgs. frozen artichoke hearts, sliced
28-oz. can peeled tomatoes, chopped and drained

Mix bread crumbs, oil, cheese and seasonings. Grease a large casserole dish; layer artichokes, tomatoes and crumb mixture in the dish, ending up with crumbs on the top. Drizzle a little water and olive oil on top, just enough to moisten. Cover and bake for 30 minutes at 350 degrees. Remove lid and continue to bake 10 to 15 minutes or until crumbs are brown. Test with knife for doneness. Serves 8.

Molly Beekley
San Antonio, TX

OVERNIGHT APPLE FRENCH TOAST

Serve it with bacon or sausage on the side, or fresh orange slices and strawberries.

1 c. brown sugar, packed
1/2 c. butter
2 T. light corn syrup
4 Granny Smith apples, peeled and sliced 1/4-inch thick
3 eggs
1 c. milk
1 t. vanilla extract
9 slices day-old French bread

In a small saucepan, combine brown sugar, butter and corn syrup; cook over low heat until thick. Pour into an ungreased 13"x9" pan, arranging apple slices on top of syrup. In a mixing bowl, beat eggs, milk and vanilla. Dip French bread in egg mixture and arrange over top of apple slices. Cover and refrigerate overnight. Remove from refrigerator 30 minutes before baking and uncover. Bake at 350 degrees for 35 to 40 minutes or until the top of the bread is browned.

Sauce:
1 c. applesauce
10-oz. jar apple jelly
1/2 t. cinnamon
1/8 t. cloves

Combine sauce ingredients and cook over medium heat until jelly is melted. Serve French toast with apple slices up and spoon the warm sauce on top. Yum!

Diane Sullivan
Gowrie, IA

Artichoke & Tomato Casserole

Rise & Shine

This year, go all out...plan a big open house for all your friends and family! Decorate the house, inside and out. Set a holiday mood with candles glowing everywhere and the scent of cinnamon pine cones roasting in a cozy fire. Put everyone in the holiday spirit by singing along (loudly!) to your favorite Christmas songs. Fill your table with taste-tempting treats...like our festive shrimp dip, tangy meatballs and scrumptious apple cake with warm vanilla sauce. You'll have so much fun, you'll plan to have open houses again and again... and create a new holiday tradition!

GLÖGGI

A Finnish holiday tradition.

1 bottle dry red wine
1 c. Madeira wine
1 T. cardamom
1 cinnamon stick
zest of 1/2 lemon
1/4 c. brown sugar, packed
1/4 c. whole blanched almonds
1/2 c. raisins

Combine red wine and Madeira in a saucepan. Add spices and bring to a simmer over low heat. Add lemon zest and sugar. Stir to dissolve the sugar, then strain to remove spices. Divide raisins and almonds into serving cups. Pour wine over raisins and almonds and serve in mugs or glasses with a spoon. Very warm and yummy!

Mari Thompson
Helsinki, Finland

Tie a pretty bow on the handle of all your party mugs!

CHEESE STRIPS

A great make-ahead appetizer.

1/2 lb. sharp Cheddar cheese, shredded
6 slices bacon, cooked and crumbled
2-oz. pkg. slivered almonds (optional)
2 t. Worcestershire sauce
1 sm. onion, minced
1 c. mayonnaise
1/4 t. dry mustard
8 slices of bread

Mix cheese, bacon, almonds, Worcestershire sauce, onion, mayonnaise and mustard together. Spread onto bread slices; cut into small strips (strips can be frozen at this point). To cook: Place in 400 degree oven for 8 to 10 minutes. Yield: approximately 32 strips.

Terri Burdoff
Fairmont, WV

STUFFED MUSHROOM CAPS

This appetizer can be prepared 3 days ahead of your open house!

25 fresh mushrooms
1 sm. onion, chopped
1/4 c. margarine
1 to 1 1/2 c. mozzarella cheese, shredded
3-oz. jar bacon bits
1/2 to 1 c. fine dry bread crumbs

Rinse mushrooms and pat dry. Remove stems; set caps aside. Chop stems finely. Sauté with onion and margarine in skillet. Remove from heat. Stir in cheese, bacon bits and bread crumbs, mixing well. Spoon mixture into mushroom caps. Place on baking sheet. Bake at 350 degrees for 12 to 15 minutes or until lightly browned. May store, covered, in refrigerator for 3 days before baking.

Lisa Miller
Lorain, OH

ZUCCHINI APPETIZERS

Quick and delicious!

3 c. unpeeled zucchini, thinly sliced
1/2 t. oregano
1/2 c. onion, finely chopped
1/2 c. Parmesan cheese, grated
1 clove garlic, finely chopped
    or 1 t. garlic powder
1/2 t. seasoned salt
1 c. biscuit baking mix
1/2 t. salt
1/2 c. vegetable oil
4 eggs, slightly beaten
2 T. snipped parsley
1/8 t. black pepper

Mix all ingredients together and spread in a greased 13"x9" pan. Bake at 350 degrees until golden brown (about 25 minutes). Cut into small pieces for appetizers or large pieces for a side dish.

Susan Harvey
Red Lion, PA

MARINATED OLIVES

These olives are quite spicy and will please anyone who loves to nibble on hot foods!

6-oz. can pitted black olives, drained and rinsed
2 2 1/2-oz. jars pitted green olives, drained and rinsed
1 hot chili pepper, minced
3 cloves garlic, minced
1 t. oregano
olive oil

Combine olives, chili pepper, garlic and oregano in a jar. Cover with olive oil. Shake olives gently and let stand at room temperature overnight. Store in refrigerator and use within one week.

WEBER DUCK

No one knows where the name came from, but it's so tasty a name isn't necessary!

4-oz. pkg. blue cheese
3-oz. pkg. cream cheese
2 T. onion, grated or chopped
5-oz. jar pimento spread or dip
1 t. Worcestershire sauce

Mash blue cheese and cream cheese with fork. Add onion. Mix thoroughly and form small cake. Put in freezer or refrigerator until firm. Mix pimento spread together with Worcestershire sauce and spread over blue cheese mixture.

Susan Smith
Walnutport, PA

Open House
at
Haley's
Sunday December 20
5 'til 8
Food, Fun and Friends!

Zucchini Appetizers, Weber Duck

10-LAYER MEXICALE DIP

Only make a few hours before or it can get runny. I cut up veggies ahead and place in plastic bags; then when I want to make it, I just start layering.

16-oz. can refried beans
1 pt. sour cream, divided
1 lg. green pepper
12-oz. jar salsa
8 to 12 oz. sharp Cheddar cheese, shredded
1 lg. tomato, diced
1 med. onion (red or yellow), diced
8 to 12 oz. mozzarella cheese, shredded

Using a fork, spread refried beans on the bottom of a 9"x9" pan (or double recipe and go for a 13"x9" pan). Stir 1/2 pint of sour cream until pourable, spread over beans. Cut green pepper into thin slivers, and place half of them over sour cream. Put salsa (mild, medium or hot, your choice) in a strainer for a few minutes to drain a bit. When drained, pour over pepper slices. Spread Cheddar cheese evenly over salsa. Stir the other 1/2 pint of sour cream until pourable, spread over cheese. Add diced tomato (if it is really juicy, put in a strainer for a few minutes). Next add the rest of the green pepper slivers. Place the onions on top of the pepper slices. Top with mozzarella cheese (or a pre-packaged taco cheese).

Wendy Lee Paffenroth
Pine Island, NY

The more the merrier.
- OLD SAYING -

10-Layer Mexicale Dip

HOT BROCCOLI DIP

We like this as a baked potato topping.

1 lb. fresh broccoli or 16-oz. pkg. frozen
16 oz. pasteurized processed cheese spread
2 4-oz. cans sliced mushrooms, drained
$10^3/_4$-oz. can cream of mushroom soup
$10^3/_4$-oz. can cream of onion soup

Cook broccoli, drain and chop into bite-size pieces. Melt cheese in microwave. Stir all ingredients together into a slow cooker. Cook until hot and well blended.

Sandy Bessingpas
Kensington, MN

MARY'S REUBEN DIP

A great sandwich filling too.

3 3-oz. pkgs. corned beef, chopped
16-oz. can sauerkraut, drained
8 oz. Swiss cheese, shredded
1 c. Thousand Island dressing

Layer above in a quiche dish and bake at 350 degrees for 30 minutes. Serve with party rye slices or pumpernickel. Serves 10 to 12.

Sara Grindle
Cordova, TN

Add fun to your tableware by setting out red and green spatterware plates!

A man hath no better thing under the sun than to **Eat, and to Drink, and to Be Merry.**

~ The Bible ~
Ecclesiastes 8:15

GUACAMOLE

This one is always a winner!

2 c. (2 lg.) avocados, mashed
2 T. lemon juice or 1 T. lemon juice and 1 T. lime juice
1 tomato, diced (optional)
2 green chilies, finely chopped
1/4 t. salt
1/4 t. chili powder
1 T. onion, grated or finely chopped
1/8 t. garlic powder

Combine all ingredients. Chill and serve.

Debbie Cummons-Parker
Lakeview, OH

Instead of using bowls or dishes to serve your holiday dips, use red and green bell peppers. Easy to clean up and very festive.

CHRISTMAS SHRIMP DIP

You can substitute lobster or crab for the shrimp, and blue cheese makes a tasty difference when substituted for cream cheese!

3-oz. pkg. cream cheese, softened
1 T. mayonnaise
1 c. shrimp, minced
1/4 t. Worcestershire sauce
2 t. onion, grated
2 t. parsley, chopped
1 1/2 t. lemon juice
1/4 t. salt
3 drops hot pepper sauce

Mix cream cheese with mayonnaise. Add remaining ingredients and blend thoroughly. Allow mixture to chill for one hour so flavors will blend. Serve with crackers or potato chips. Makes 3/4 cup.

Sandy Wisneski
Ripon, WI

Guacamole, Christmas Shrimp Dip

PREPARE HOLIDAY FOODS THAT CAN BE MADE **AHEAD OF TIME.**

SOUTH STREET TORTILLA ROLL-UPS

A wonderful appetizer!

8-oz. pkg. cream cheese
1 lg. onion, chopped
8 oz. sour cream
1¼-oz. pkg. taco seasoning
8 oz. Cheddar cheese, shredded
4½-oz. can chopped green chilies, drained
2 tomatoes, chopped and drained
hot pepper sauce to taste
10 flour tortillas
Garnish: salsa and guacamole

Combine cream cheese, onion, sour cream and taco seasoning until smooth. Fold in cheese, chilies, tomatoes and hot sauce blending well. Spread mixture on tortillas, then roll tortillas. For easier cutting, refrigerate roll-ups until cream cheese mixture is firm. Slice and serve cold with salsa and guacamole.

So good!

When hosting a holiday party, encourage guests to mingle throughout your home. Set up snacks and bowls of punch, eggnog and coffee in the living room, dining room and study. Your friends will be able to enjoy your holiday decorations so much more!

FIRESIDE DELIGHT CHOCOLATE DIP

Try dipping toasted marshmallows into this rich, velvety chocolate.

3 T. butter
3 T. milk or water
2 c. sweetened cocoa mix
¼ t. instant coffee

Melt butter in small saucepan over medium heat. Add milk, cocoa and coffee. Stir briskly with whisk or wooden spoon until hot, but not boiling. Add more milk or water if needed. With wooden skewers or fondue forks, dip slices of apples, bananas, peaches, pineapples, oranges or angel food cake.

TROPICAL CHICKEN WINGS

A little different from the hot wings we usually have.

2 to 3 lbs. chicken wings, tips removed
10 oz. soy sauce
46-oz. can pineapple juice
5 cloves garlic
1 to 2 t. ginger
1 c. brown sugar, packed

Parboil chicken for 20 minutes. Combine remaining ingredients in a large bowl, then add chicken. Cover and refrigerate overnight. Discard marinade. Bake at 400 degrees for 5 minutes, turn wings and bake 5 minutes more.

Lisa Card
Gardner, MA

South Street Tortilla Roll-Ups

Baked Brie with Tomato Sauce

RUDOLPH'S NOSE HERBAL CHILI BALL

Make ahead of time to allow flavors to blend.

8-oz. pkg. cream cheese, softened
8 oz. sharp Cheddar cheese, shredded
2 t. chili powder
1/2 t. thyme
1/4 t. rosemary
1 t. poppy seeds
1 t. sesame seeds
2 t. grated onion
1 garlic clove, minced
1 t. sherry
chili powder to coat

Mix or process cheeses together. Add remaining ingredients and beat until smooth. Refrigerate this mixture for 30 minutes or until the mixture can be handled easily. Shape into a ball or a log. Roll in chili powder until coated. Wrap in wax paper, then place in a plastic bag. Refrigerate at least 24 hours before serving. Serve with crackers. Makes a one-pound cheese ball.

Judy Hand
Centre Hall, PA

MUSHROOM LOGS

Delicious tidbits.

2 8-oz. cans crescent dinner rolls
8-oz. pkg. cream cheese, softened
2 4-oz. cans mushroom pieces, drained and chopped
1 t. seasoned salt
1 bunch scallions, chopped
1 T. Worcestershire sauce
1 t. lemon pepper
1 egg, beaten
2 T. poppy seeds (optional)

Separate dough into 4 rectangles, pressing seams together. Combine cream cheese with mushrooms, salt, scallions, Worcestershire sauce and lemon pepper. Spread evenly over rectangles. Roll into logs, starting with long side of rectangle. Pinch seams. Brush with egg, sprinkle with poppy seeds. Cut into one-inch pieces. Place on ungreased cookie sheet, seam side down. Bake at 375 degrees for 10 to 12 minutes.

Ann Fehr
Collegeville, PA

BAKED BRIE WITH TOMATO SAUCE

There's something about this Brie that brings out the fiercest of appetites!

1 frozen pastry shell, thawed
8 oz. Brie, chilled
1 T. olive oil
1 med. onion, chopped
2 garlic cloves, crushed
14 1/2-oz. can tomatoes, drained and chopped
1/2 T. fresh basil, chopped
1 T. fresh parsley, chopped
1 small bay leaf
salt and pepper to taste
1 T. raisins
2 T. pine nuts

With a rolling pin, flatten the pastry shell and roll out to a size that will completely cover the cheese. Wrap the cheese in the pastry, tucking the ends in snugly underneath. Make sure there are no openings in the shell. Chill the wrapped cheese for an hour. While cheese is chilling, heat the olive oil in a skillet and sauté the onion and garlic until tender. Stir in the remaining ingredients. Allow to simmer for 15 minutes. Place chilled cheese in a 450 degree oven and bake for 15 to 20 minutes or until browned. Cool 15 minutes. Spoon tomato sauce onto a serving plate and place the cheese on top, discarding the bay leaf. Serve with crackers.

JUST SMILE & TELL YOUR GUESTS IT'S A CREOLE DISH: BLACKENED CHICKEN?

Santa Fe Pie

SANTA FE PIE
Just slice and eat!

10-oz. pkg. deep-dish pie crust mix
$2^3/4$ t. chili powder, divided
10 oz. ground chuck
$1/2$ c. onion, chopped
1 c. water
$1^1/2$ t. taco sauce
3 T. taco seasoning mix
$1/3$ c. ripe olives, pitted
$1/2$ c. Monterey Jack cheese,
    shredded
$1/2$ c. Cheddar cheese, shredded
2 T. chopped green chilies
4 med. eggs
1 c. plus 2 T. milk
1 T. all-purpose flour
$1/8$ t. salt
$1/8$ t. red pepper

Prepare pie crust according to package directions, adding $3/4$ teaspoon chili powder to mixture. Roll out dough and place in pie pan, bake as directed. Brown ground chuck and onion, draining excess fat. Add water, taco sauce, taco seasoning mix and $1^1/2$ teaspoons chili powder to beef mixture; simmer 15 to 20 minutes. Blend in olives; remove from heat. Sprinkle half of the cheese in bottom of pie pan over baked pie crust. On top of cheese, layer beef, remaining cheese and chilies. In a large mixing bowl, beat eggs lightly; add milk. In a separate mixing bowl, combine flour, salt, red pepper and $1/2$ teaspoon of chili powder. Add a small amount of the egg mixture to the flour mixture and whip until smooth. Add flour mixture to remaining egg-milk mixture, blending well. Pour mixture over pie and bake at 375 degrees for 30 to 35 minutes.

SEAFOOD CASSEROLE
Delicious!

$1/2$ c. green pepper, chopped
$1/2$ c. onion, chopped
$1/2$ c. celery, chopped
8 oz. fresh mushrooms, sliced
$1/2$ c. margarine
$2/3$ c. all-purpose flour
$1/2$ t. garlic, minced
$1/2$ t. salt
$1/4$ t. paprika
$1/8$ teaspoon red pepper
$10^3/4$-oz. can cream of shrimp
    soup
2 c. milk
16 oz. crabmeat
2 lbs. raw shrimp, peeled
8-oz. can water chestnuts
2 T. butter, softened
$1/2$ c. sharp Cheddar cheese,
    shredded
$1/2$ c. fresh bread crumbs

Sauté pepper, onion, celery and mushrooms in margarine. Stir in flour and cook one minute. Add seasonings. Stir in soup and milk. Continue to stir until thickened. Combine crabmeat, shrimp and water chestnuts in a 2-quart casserole. Pour sauce over seafood mixture. Combine butter, cheese and crumbs. Sprinkle over casserole. Bake at 350 degrees for 30 to 35 minutes. Serves 8 to 10.

Leslie Carpenter
Richmond, VA

TANGY BARBECUED MEATBALLS
A hearty appetizer for any party!

Meatballs:
2 lbs. ground round
1 c. cornflake crumbs
$1/3$ c. parsley flakes
2 eggs
2 T. soy sauce
$1/4$ t. pepper
$1/2$ t. garlic powder
$1/3$ c. catsup
2 T. instant minced onion

Sauce:
16-oz. can jellied cranberry sauce
12-oz. bottle chili sauce, regular
2 T. brown sugar, packed
1 T. lemon juice

Mix ingredients and form into small meatballs. Put in 13"x9" pan. Set aside. In saucepan over medium heat, mix sauce ingredients, stirring until smooth and cranberry sauce is melted. Pour sauce over meatballs and bake uncovered for 45 minutes at 350 degrees.

Linda Zell
Delavan, WI

Wrap popcorn balls in colorful plastic wrap and tie with a festive bow. Stack them in a basket near your door to give guests as they leave or as quick gifts for the mailman, paper carrier or strolling carolers!

DROPPED TEA CAKES

This recipe makes 6 dozen delicious tea cakes...perfect for an open house!

1 c. butter, softened
2¼ c. sugar
4 eggs
4½ c. all-purpose flour
1 t. baking soda
1 t. baking powder
½ t. nutmeg
¼ c. buttermilk
1 t. lemon extract
1 t. vanilla extract
1 t. almond extract

Cream butter. Gradually add sugar, beating well at medium speed. Add eggs, beating well. Combine flour, baking soda, baking powder and nutmeg. Add to creamed mixture alternately with buttermilk, mixing well. Stir in flavors. Drop dough by tablespoonfuls onto greased cookie sheets. Bake at 375 degrees for 8 to 10 minutes, or until lightly browned. Cool. Yields 6 dozen.

Rosa Stickland
Bradley, AR

APPLE CAKE

Drizzle warm vanilla sauce over cake slices.

Cake:
1 c. oil
2 c. sugar
2 eggs
1 t. vanilla extract
1 t. salt
1 t. baking soda
2 t. baking powder
2½ c. all-purpose flour
3 c. apples, chopped

Topping:
⅓ c. brown sugar, packed
1 t. cinnamon
½ c. nuts, chopped

Vanilla Sauce:
1 c. sugar
2 T. all-purpose flour
1½ c. whipping cream
½ c. butter
2 t. vanilla extract

For cake, beat oil, sugar, eggs and vanilla together. Blend in dry ingredients, then stir in apples. Press into a lightly oiled 13"x9" pan. For topping, combine all ingredients and sprinkle over cake. Bake at 350 degrees for 35 to 45 minutes. For vanilla sauce, blend sugar and flour together in a saucepan. Whisk in whipping cream. Add butter and cook over medium heat, whisking often, until thickened. Add vanilla and stir. Serve cake warm with vanilla sauce.

Pam Hilton
Centerburg, OH

Apple Cake

For a really pretty centerpiece, place a white three-wick candle on a round platter. Place individual magnolia leaves flat around the candle with stem end in toward the candle. Alternate golden and red delicious apples on top of the magnolia leaves. Fill around the candle and in between the apples with boxwood and rose hips.

Well, maybe just a teensy little slice...

Bountiful Banquet

Gather the family around the table, carve the turkey and pass the stuffing...it's Christmas Day! After the meal, linger at the table and enjoy a second helping of dessert with a cup of coffee. The dishes can wait!

Herb-Seasoned Spinach Puffs, Curried Chicken Canapés, Marinated Broccoli & Mushroom Appetizer

MARINATED BROCCOLI & MUSHROOM APPETIZER

I have been serving this recipe at family functions for the past eight years. It is very tasty!

1 T. lemon juice
2 t. tarragon vinegar
1 t. Dijon mustard
1 T. plus 1 t. olive oil
2 t. fresh parsley, minced
1/4 c. fresh chives or 2 chopped scallions
1/2 t. each: salt and fennel seed
1/8 t. pepper, freshly ground
2 c. halved mushrooms, blanched
1 1/2 c. broccoli flowerets, blanched

In measuring cup or small bowl, combine lemon juice, vinegar and mustard. Gradually add oil, stirring constantly, until mixture becomes thick and creamy; add parsley, chives or scallions, salt, fennel and pepper and mix well. Set aside. In a medium bowl (nonmetallic), combine mushrooms, broccoli and dressing. Toss to lightly coat the vegetables. Cover with plastic wrap and refrigerate overnight. It is very important to let sit at least 10 hours so the flavors can mellow and the vegetables soak up all of the flavor. Yields 4 servings.

Jeanne Calkins
Midland, MI

110

CURRIED CHICKEN CANAPÉS

You may try these with sourdough or rye bread, too.

1 c. cooked chicken, minced
1 c. mayonnaise
3/4 c. Monterey Jack cheese, shredded
1/3 c. almonds, ground
1/4 c. fresh parsley, minced
1 t. dried dill weed
2 lg. shallots, minced
2 t. fresh lemon juice
1 1/2 to 2 t. curry powder
1/8 t. hot pepper sauce
60 rounds of thinly sliced whole wheat bread
1/2 lb. slivered almonds

Combine all ingredients except bread and almonds in large bowl and blend well. Cover and refrigerate until ready to serve. Preheat oven to 450 degrees. Spread 1 1/2 teaspoons of chicken mixture on each round, mounding in center. Top with slivered almonds. Place on baking sheet and bake about 5 minutes or until sizzling. Serve hot.

HERB-SEASONED SPINACH PUFFS

Add a spicy mustard sauce for dipping.

2 10-oz. pkgs. frozen chopped spinach, thawed and drained
2 c. herb-seasoned stuffing mix
1 c. Parmesan cheese, grated
6 eggs, lightly beaten
1/3 c. butter, softened

Drain and squeeze spinach until all liquid is removed. Combine with stuffing mix, cheese, eggs and butter, mixing well. Roll into one-inch balls and place on a lightly oiled baking sheet. Cover with foil and chill overnight. Bake at 350 degrees for 10 minutes or until thoroughly heated. Place on paper towels to absorb excess liquid. Makes 4 1/2 dozen puffs.

Creamy Wild Rice Soup

CREAMY WILD RICE SOUP

Terrific served with warm pumpernickel bread and herb butter.

4 1/2 c. fresh mushrooms, sliced
1 c. sweet onion, chopped
1 c. celery, chopped
4 T. butter
1/2 c. all-purpose flour
4 c. chicken broth
1 c. half-and-half
1 1/2 c. wild rice, cooked
1 T. fresh marjoram
salt and pepper to taste

Combine mushrooms, onion and celery with butter in a Dutch oven. Cook over medium heat until vegetables are tender. Sprinkle flour over vegetables, stirring well. Stirring constantly, add broth and simmer until thick. Reduce heat and add half-and-half, rice, marjoram, salt and pepper. Continue to cook over low heat until thoroughly heated. Serves 6.

So now is come our joyfull'st feast; Let every man be jolly....
— GEORGE WITHER —

★ Celebrate ★ Celebrate ★

CHRISTMAS LUNCHEON CRABMEAT BISQUE

Or make a shrimp bisque by replacing crab with 1 1/2 cups cooked, deveined shrimp.

6 T. butter
4 T. green pepper, finely chopped
4 T. onion, finely chopped
1 scallion, chopped
2 T. fresh parsley, chopped
1 1/2 c. fresh mushrooms, sliced
2 T. all-purpose flour
1 c. milk
1 t. salt
1/8 t. white pepper
1/8 t. hot pepper sauce
1 1/2 c. half-and-half
1 1/2 c. cooked crabmeat
3 T. dry sherry

Heat 4 tablespoons butter in a skillet. Add next 5 ingredients and sauté until soft. In saucepan, heat remaining 2 tablespoons butter and stir in flour. Add milk and cook, stirring until thickened and smooth. Stir in salt, pepper and hot pepper sauce. Add sautéed vegetables and half-and-half. Bring to a boil, stirring; reduce heat. Add crabmeat, simmer uncovered for 5 minutes. Stir in sherry just prior to serving. Serves 4.

*Judy Hand
Centre Hall, PA*

MARY ELIZABETH'S HELPFUL GUIDE TO STORING LETTUCE & GREENS

Try to choose the freshest-looking greens. Discard any wilted or damaged leaves, then wash the "keepers" under cold running water. You can also clean them by swirling them around in a bowl of cold water.

Dry greens thoroughly! Pat dry with a dish towel, paper towels or a salad spinner (no hair dryers, please). Wet greens make for a tasteless salad as dressings will not cling to wet leaves... all your yummy dressing will end up in the bottom of the bowl!

After greens are completely dry, wrap them in a clean cloth dish towel or paper towels, then store them in a plastic container or large plastic bag. Refrigerate at least 30 minutes to crisp. Greens should stay fresh & crisp up to 4 days.

Always tear lettuce and greens by hand into bite-size pieces. Cutting with a knife can lead to brown edges on the leaves. A knife can be used, though, when your recipe calls for shredded greens.

Your pastry blender is perfect for slicing avocados or hard-boiled eggs.

Spinach Salad

SPINACH SALAD

Delicious and your friends will all want the recipe for the dressing!

fresh spinach leaves
4 oz. feta cheese, crumbled
1/2 c. walnuts, chopped
1 avocado, sliced
3 to 4 T. real bacon bits
1/2 red onion, cut into thin rings
1/2 c. red pepper, cut into strips
1 tomato, chopped

Using a large bowl, fill with spinach leaves. Add all other ingredients to bowl. Toss salad with sweet and sour dressing. Great for spinach salads and pasta salads.

Dressing:
1 1/2 c. oil
1/2 c. red wine vinegar
3 T. sugar
1 t. chili powder
2 t. onion, grated (optional)
1 t. seasoned salt
garlic to taste
2 to 3 T. Worcestershire sauce

Shake well. Pour enough dressing to cover spinach leaves. Toss.

Barb McFaden
Missoula, MT

CRUNCHY GRANNY SMITH SALAD

A refreshing combination!

1 lg. head red leaf lettuce, torn
2 Granny Smith apples, cored, sliced and cut in half
4 oz. Swiss cheese, shredded
4 oz. cashews, chopped
1 c. oil
1 T. onion, minced
1 t. dry mustard
1/2 c. sugar
1/3 c. vinegar
2 t. poppy seed

Layer the first 4 ingredients in bowl. Mix the remaining ingredients in blender for poppy seed dressing. Pour dressing over salad.

Gloria Kaufmann
Orrville, OH

COLORFUL CHRISTMAS SALAD

The one dish children always remember.

3-oz. pkg. lime gelatin
1 c. crushed pineapple, drained
1/2 c. mayonnaise
8-oz. pkg. cream cheese, softened
1/2 c. walnuts, chopped
3-oz. pkg. cranberry gelatin
1/2 c. cranberry sauce

Prepare lime gelatin as directed on package and chill until slightly thickened. Fold in pineapple. Pour into an 8-inch pan or mold and chill until firm. Add mayonnaise to cream cheese, mixing until well blended. Add nuts and spread over molded gelatin layer. Chill until firm. Prepare cranberry gelatin and add cranberry sauce. Pour over cheese mixture and chill until firm. Remove from mold by placing mold in hot water for a few minutes; then invert onto a serving platter.

TRIPLE CRANBERRY SAUCE

Pretty served in a footed glass compote.

1 c. frozen cranberry juice
    concentrate
1/3 c. sugar
12-oz. pkg. fresh or frozen
    cranberries, rinsed and drained
1/2 c. dried cranberries
3 T. orange marmalade
2 T. fresh orange juice
2 t. orange zest, minced
1/4 t. allspice

Combine cranberry juice, sugar and cranberries in heavy medium saucepan. Bring to a boil over high heat, stirring often until berries begin to soften and fresh berries begin to pop, about 7 minutes. Remove from heat and stir in orange marmalade, orange juice, orange zest and allspice. Cool completely. Cover and chill until cold, about 2 hours. Can be made 3 days ahead. Keep refrigerated. Makes about 2 1/2 cups.

Cindy Layton
Cape Girardeau, MO

OUT-OF-THIS-WORLD ROLLS

My favorite recipe...because after I began using this recipe I had perfect rolls every time. My husband no longer says, "I wish you could make rolls like Mom's." Now I do!

2 T. yeast
1/2 c. sugar
1 1/2 c. warm water
1/2 c. shortening
3 eggs, beaten
5 c. all-purpose flour
2 t. salt
butter, melted

Dissolve yeast and 1/2 teaspoon sugar in 1/2 cup warm water; set aside. In a large mixing bowl, cream shortening and remaining sugar. Add eggs, remaining water and yeast mixture. Beat with an electric mixer or a heavy-duty whisk. Sift flour and salt together and add to yeast mixture in 3 batches. Continue beating until glossy in texture. Dough will be sticky; do not add additional flour. Cover and set bowl in a warm place; let rise one hour. Mix down with hands and cover bowl with a plastic bag that has been oiled inside. Secure bag around bowl with a rubber band to close tightly. Cool overnight in the refrigerator. Dough will continue to rise; make sure bowl is large enough to allow for growth of dough. About 2 hours before ready to bake, remove from refrigerator and shape into rolls. Place in a greased baking pan, rolls touching. Brush tops with melted butter; let rise until doubled. Bake at 350 degrees for 15 to 20 minutes. Makes 3 to 4 dozen rolls.

Linda Murdock
Selah, WA

Colorful Christmas Salad

If you substitute milk for water in your bread recipe, you'll get a finer texture. Water gives bread a coarser texture.

Pork Crown Roast with Fruit Glaze, Stuffed Zucchini, Out-of-This-World Rolls (recipe on page 113)

PORK CROWN ROAST WITH FRUIT GLAZE

The crowning glory of your Christmas groaning board.

1^1/$_2$ t. fennel seed, crushed
1^1/$_2$ t. onion powder
1 t. salt
1 t. pepper
8-lb. pork crown roast
vegetable oil

Combine first 4 ingredients in a small bowl. Rub this mixture on all sides of the roast, cover and refrigerate overnight. Brush the roast lightly with oil and insert a meat thermometer. Cover the bone ends with foil and place roast on a rack in a 325 degree oven. Roast until thermometer reads 165 degrees. Allow to stand for 10 minutes before carving.

Fruit Glaze:
^{1}/$_2$ c. dried apricot halves
^{1}/$_2$ c. dried peach halves
^{3}/$_4$ c. apple juice, divided
^{1}/$_4$ t. cardamom
2 t. corn starch
1 c. seedless green grapes
1 c. seedless red grapes

In a 1^1/$_2$-quart casserole, combine fruit, ^{1}/$_2$ cup of apple juice and cardamom. Cover casserole dish and microwave on high power for 6 minutes or until fruit begins to fill out. In a separate bowl, combine corn starch and remaining apple juice, stirring well. Add to fruit mixture and microwave on high power for 2 minutes, or until thick. Add grapes, stir gently and spoon as a garnish around pork roast. Makes 8 to 10 servings.

Cathy Moore
Powell, OH

A quick and easy seasoning mix is six parts salt to one part pepper. Keep it handy in a large shaker close to the stove.

"Better a good dinner than a fine coat."
— French Proverb

STUFFED ZUCCHINI
A great way to get kids to like zucchini!

2 med. zucchini
3 T. onion, chopped
1 slice bacon, chopped
1/2 c. fresh mushrooms, sliced or
    4 oz. canned (optional)
1/2 c. tomato, chopped
1/4 c. chicken broth
1/2 t. dried basil leaves
1/2 t. thyme
1/8 t. pepper
1 c. seasoned bread crumbs
    (for stuffing)

Steam zucchini 15 minutes. Slice lengthwise, remove pulp and reserve. Fry onion and bacon until onion is translucent. Add mushrooms, tomato and reserved pulp. Cook 5 minutes, stirring occasionally. Add broth and seasonings; bring to a boil. Add bread crumbs and remove from heat. Fill zucchini shells with mixture. Bake at 350 degrees for 25 minutes.

Julie Carwile
Blackstone, VA

SAUSAGE STUFFING
A great recipe from one of the best cooks we know!

1/4 c. butter
5 c. French bread, cubed
1/2 lb. pork sausage
1 sm. onion, chopped
1/3 c. celery, thinly sliced
1 med. apple, cored and chopped
1/2 c. pecans or walnuts, chopped
1/3 c. chicken broth

Melt butter over medium heat in a large skillet. Add bread cubes, stirring well to coat. Over medium heat, continue to cook until bread is lightly toasted. Place in a mixing bowl and set aside. Using the same skillet, cook sausage over medium heat, breaking up and stirring until completely done. Add onion and celery, cooking until tender. Remove from heat and add to bread crumb mixture. Add apple and nuts, mixing thoroughly. Add broth. In a greased 1 1/2-quart casserole dish, bake dressing covered for 30 minutes at 350 degrees. Remove cover from casserole and bake 15 to 25 minutes or until thoroughly heated.

Carol Sheets
Gooseberry Patch

THE JUICIEST-EVER ROAST TURKEY
This turkey's a winner!

1/4 c. dry mustard
2 T. Worcestershire sauce
1/4 to 1/2 t. cider vinegar
2 1/2 T. olive oil
1 t. salt
1/8 t. pepper, freshly ground
1 turkey (about 10 pounds),
    thawed
1 onion
1 to 2 stalks celery
fresh parsley
2 pieces bacon
1/2 c. butter

In a small bowl, combine dry mustard, Worcestershire sauce, vinegar, olive oil, salt and pepper. Stir until a soft paste forms. Paint mixture over turkey, inside and out, a few hours or the day before cooking turkey. Stuff turkey with onion, celery and parsley. Lay bacon across the breast and tuck chunks of butter in the crevice between the drumstick and the body. Soak a piece of cheesecloth in olive oil and lay it over the turkey, which you put in an uncovered roaster. Use one to 2 cups stock or use chicken broth for basting through the cheesecloth during the roasting. Insert meat thermometer into thickest part of thigh, making sure thermometer does not touch bone. Bake at 325 degrees about 3 1/2 to 4 hours or until meat thermometer registers 180 degrees. Let stand 20 minutes before carving.

Karyl Bannister
West Southport, ME

The Juiciest-Ever Roast Turkey, Sausage Stuffing, Triple Cranberry Sauce (recipe on page 113)

I HAD NO IDEA SANTA WAS SUCH A GOOD COOK!

SPORE

BAKED APPLES

This is a great old-fashioned recipe you can try for a special treat or side dish with pork or ham!

1/3 c. golden raisins
1/3 c. dark raisins
1/4 c. water
2 T. bourbon
6 tart apples
4 T. butter (1/2 stick)
2 T. all-purpose flour
1/2 c. brown sugar, packed
1/2 t. vanilla extract

Preheat oven to 425 degrees. In small saucepan, combine raisins, water and bourbon. Cook over low heat, stirring occasionally, until raisins are plumped. Remove from heat. Core apples and peel about halfway down. Spoon raisins into center of each apple. In small saucepan, melt butter; stir in flour until smooth. Stir in brown sugar and vanilla; spread over apples. Bake 15 minutes or until crust is set. Reduce temperature to 350 degrees and bake apples until tender, about 30 minutes. Serve warm.

Juanita Williams
Jacksonville, OR

SCALLOPED SWEET POTATOES

Hearty, healthy and a family favorite.

4 lbs. sweet potatoes, peeled and sliced lengthwise
1 c. apple juice
salt and pepper to taste
1 c. light brown sugar, packed
1/4 c. butter

Place sweet potatoes in a 6-cup baking dish. Add salt and pepper to juice; pour over potatoes. Bake, covered, in a 400 degree oven for 40 minutes. Reduce the heat to 350 degrees and bake, covered, 30 minutes more. Sprinkle potatoes with brown sugar and dot with butter. Bake, uncovered, 10 minutes longer. Serves 8.

FARMHOUSE HONEY-WHEAT BREAD

Nutritious, delicious and freezes well.

1 1/2 c. water
1 c. sm. curd cottage cheese
1/2 c. honey
1/4 c. butter
5 1/2 to 6 c. all-purpose flour
1 c. whole wheat flour
2 T. sugar
1 T. salt
2 pkgs. active dry yeast
1 egg

In a saucepan heat water, cottage cheese, honey and butter until very warm, 120 degrees. Combine warm liquid with 2 cups flour and remaining ingredients, beating with an electric mixer for 2 minutes. By hand, add enough flour to make a stiff dough and knead on a well-floured surface until smooth and elastic. Place in an oiled bowl, cover and allow to rise until doubled in bulk, about one hour. Punch down and shape into 2 loaves; place in 2 oiled 9"x5" loaf pans. Cover and allow to rise for 45 minutes or until doubled in size. Bake at 350 degrees for 30 minutes or until loaves sound hollow when tapped.

Mary Murray
Gooseberry Patch

Farmhouse Honey-Wheat Bread, Baked Apples, Scalloped Sweet Potatoes

Where our work is, there let our JOY be.

~ Tertullian (c.160-240)

A few drops of lemon juice in the water will whiten boiled potatoes.

Cheesy Lima & Tomato Casserole, Company Potatoes

CHEESY LIMA & TOMATO CASSEROLE

Try this one with spinach instead of lima beans. Also very delicious!

¼ c. onion, minced
2 T. butter
4 c. canned tomatoes, crushed
2 10-oz. pkgs. frozen lima beans, cooked and drained
2 t. chili powder
1 t. salt
3 T. all-purpose flour
¼ c. water
2 c. Cheddar cheese, shredded

Cook onion in butter. Add tomatoes, limas, chili powder and salt. Simmer uncovered for 10 minutes. Blend flour into water to make a paste. Stir into vegetables and cook over low heat to thicken. Put into a casserole dish and top with cheese. Bake at 350 degrees for 20 minutes.

Judy Borecky
Escondido, CA

COMPANY POTATOES

Company potatoes can be made days ahead of time and refrigerated. Perfect for a family gathering!

5 lbs. potatoes
2 c. sour cream
8 oz. cream cheese
½ c. margarine or butter

Wash, peel and cook potatoes until soft. Combine potatoes, sour cream, cream cheese and margarine. Beat until smooth. Spoon into a greased 2-quart casserole dish. Bake at 375 degrees for 45 minutes or until bubbly. The depth of the casserole dish may cause a variance in the baking time.

Valerie Bryan
Woodbridge, CT

CHRISTMAS PLUM PUDDING

Prepare two weeks before Christmas Day.

1/2 c. dates, chopped
1/2 c. golden raisins
1/2 c. brandy
2 c. all-purpose flour
1 t. baking soda
1 t. cinnamon
1/2 t. nutmeg
1/2 t. salt
1 c. butter, softened
1 c. dark brown sugar, packed
1/2 c. molasses
3 eggs
1/4 c. milk
1/4 c. brandy
1 c. almonds, slivered
2/3 c. coconut, flaked
1 c. plain bread crumbs

AM I DREAMING ?

Soak together the first 3 ingredients the night before making pudding. On the next day, combine and sift together next 5 ingredients. Cream butter and brown sugar well. Add molasses and eggs; beat in flour mixture and milk alternately. Add brandy. Stir in dates, raisins, almonds, coconut and bread crumbs. Pour into a greased 6-cup mold. Cover with buttered wax paper, tie with string and cover again with foil. Place on rack in large pot. Add water to just below rack. Cover and steam for 3 hours. Keep adding water to pan so it does not go dry. Cool and store at room temperature until Christmas Day. To serve, steam 2 hours, remove and cool 10 minutes. Loosen edges and invert onto plate. Decorate with artificial greenery and serve with brandy butter.

Brandy Butter:
1 c. powdered sugar
1/2 c. butter, softened
1 T. brandy
1 T. rum

Beat sugar and butter. Beat in brandy and rum and chill.

Joyce Milstead
Dallastown, PA

Granny's Apple-Cranberry Tart

GRANNY'S APPLE-CRANBERRY TART

The perfect pie for Christmas dinner.

Crust:
2/3 c. walnuts, chopped
1 c. all-purpose flour
2 T. sugar
1/4 t. cinnamon
1/4 t. salt
1/3 c. cold butter, sliced into
    pieces
2 to 3 T. ice water

Filling:
2 T. all-purpose flour
1/3 c. plus 2 T. sugar
3 Granny Smith apples, cored,
    peeled and thinly sliced
1 c. fresh cranberries
1/4 c. orange juice
2 t. orange zest, grated
1 t. corn starch
Garnish: whipped cream and
    cinnamon

To make the crust, process walnuts in a food processor until coarsely ground. Add flour, sugar, cinnamon and salt and process until just mixed. Add butter and pulse until mixture resembles small coarse crumbs. With food processor running, add the ice water to form dough. Remove dough, form into a ball and flatten into a circle. Wrap in plastic and refrigerate for 30 minutes. While crust is chilling, preheat oven to 375 degrees and prepare filling. In mixing bowl, combine flour and 2 tablespoons sugar. Toss with apples and set aside. Roll out dough and pat into a 9-inch tart pan. Spoon in apple mixture and bake for 25 minutes. While baking, combine cranberries, orange juice, orange zest, corn starch and remaining sugar. Cook cranberry mixture over medium-low heat until it boils and thickens. Remove from heat and spoon over baked apple tart. Bake for another 10 minutes or until apples are tender. Allow to cool. Serve with a dollop of whipped cream and sprinkle of cinnamon.

Mary Murray
Gooseberry Patch

MULLED CRANBERRY SYLLABUB

Float a colorful orange slice in each mug.

1 qt. cranberry juice cocktail
18-oz. can pineapple juice
3 cinnamon sticks
1 t. whole allspice
1 t. whole cloves
1/8 t. nutmeg
1/2 t. orange extract
1/2 t. lemon extract
cinnamon sticks for garnish

Combine first 6 ingredients in large saucepan. Bring mixture to a boil; reduce heat and simmer, covered, 20 minutes. Remove from heat; strain. Stir in extracts. Serve hot with sticks of cinnamon. Serves 8.

RASPBERRY TRUFFLE CHEESECAKE

Garnish with whipped cream, raspberries and mint leaves...beautiful!

1 1/2 c. chocolate sandwich cookies, crushed (about 18 cookies)
2 T. butter, melted
4 8-oz. pkgs. cream cheese, softened
1 1/4 c. sugar
3 lg. eggs
1 c. sour cream
1 t. almond extract
2 6-oz. pkgs. chocolate chips
1/3 c. seedless raspberry preserves
1/4 c. whipping cream

For crust, combine cookies and butter. Press into bottom of a 9-inch springform pan. To prepare the filling, combine 3 packages of cream cheese with sugar, mixing at medium speed until well blended. Add eggs, one at a time, mixing after each. Blend in sour cream and extract. Pour over crust. Melt one package of chocolate chips and combine with remaining package of cream cheese. Add preserves and mix well. Drop rounded tablespoonfuls of chocolate cream cheese batter over plain batter. Do not swirl! Bake at 325 degrees for one hour and 20 minutes. Let cool and remove from pan. To prepare topping, melt remaining chocolate chips with whipping cream over low heat, stirring until smooth. Spread over cheesecake and let some drizzle over the sides. Chill for 4 hours. Serves 12 to 14.

Deborah Hilton
Oswego, NY

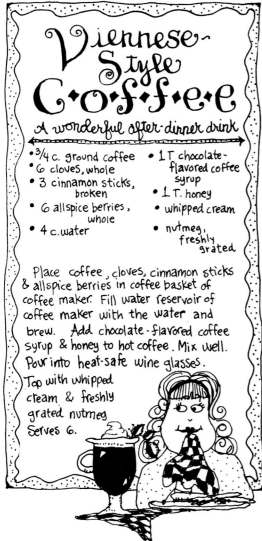

Viennese-Style Coffee

A wonderful after-dinner drink

- 3/4 c. ground coffee
- 6 cloves, whole
- 3 cinnamon sticks, broken
- 6 allspice berries, whole
- 4 c. water
- 1 T. chocolate-flavored coffee syrup
- 1 T. honey
- whipped cream
- nutmeg, freshly grated

Place coffee, cloves, cinnamon sticks & allspice berries in coffee basket of coffee maker. Fill water reservoir of coffee maker with the water and brew. Add chocolate-flavored coffee syrup & honey to hot coffee. Mix well. Pour into heat-safe wine glasses. Top with whipped cream & freshly grated nutmeg. Serves 6.

Viennese-Style Coffee, Raspberry Truffle Cheesecake

FAMILY MEMORY ALBUM

(shown on pages 8 and 9)

- paper-backed fusible web
- scrap of homespun fabric
- cotton batting
- assorted colors of felt for appliqués
- 10"x11½" photo album with center rings
- one yard of fabric to cover album
- 6½"x8¼" piece of blue felt for sky
- 7¾"x9¼" piece of red felt for border
- assorted colors of embroidery floss
- tracing paper
- hot glue gun
- poster board

Refer to Embroidery Stitches, page 135, and use 3 strands of floss for all stitching.

1. Using the patterns, page 138, follow *Making Appliqués*, page 134, to make one house from homespun; one each of the snowbank, banner, roof and chimney cap from batting; one each of the door, wreath, heart, bow, star and chimney from felt; 2 each (one in reverse) of the tree, window and window frame from felt; and 4 tabs from felt.

2. For the cover, draw around the open album on the wrong side of the album fabric; cut out 3-inches outside the drawn line.

3. Fuse the snowbank to the sky piece. Center the sky piece on the red border; work Blanket Stitches along the edges of the sky and snowbank. Referring to **Fig. 1**, center the border on the fabric and work Running Stitches along the edges of the border.

Fig. 1

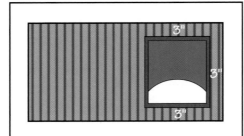

4. Arrange and fuse the remaining appliqués on the album cover.

5. Trace the message, page 138, onto tracing paper. Center the message over the banner and pin in place. Stitching through the tracing paper, work Running Stitches over the message and along the edges of the banner. Carefully remove the tracing paper. Embellish the design with French Knots for snow and decorations on the wreath, Straight Stitches for accents on the trees, Blanket Stitches along the edges of the house and door, and Cross Stitches for the windowpanes.

6. Center the album on the wrong side of the cover with the design under the front of the album. Fold the corners of the fabric diagonally over the corners of the album; glue in place. Fold the short edges of the fabric over the side edges of the album; glue in place. Fold the long edges of the fabric over the top and bottom edges of the album, trimming the fabric to fit ¼-inch under the binding hardware; glue in place.

7. Cut two 3-inch-wide fabric strips ½-inch shorter than the height of the album. Press the ends of each strip ¼-inch to the wrong side. With one long edge of each strip tucked ¼-inch under the hardware, center and glue one strip along each side of the binding hardware.

8. To line the inside of the album, cut 2 pieces of poster board one inch smaller than the front of the album. Cut 2 pieces of fabric 2-inches larger than the poster board pieces.

9. Center one poster board piece on the wrong side of one fabric piece. Fold the corners of the fabric piece diagonally over the corners of the poster board; glue in place. Fold the edges of the fabric over the edges of the poster board; glue in place. Repeat with remaining poster board and fabric.

10. Glue the liners to the insides of the album cover.

BABY'S FIRST ORNAMENT

(shown on page 10)

- stamp pad
- piece of muslin
- tracing paper
- cotton batting
- homespun fabric
- red and green embroidery floss
- polyester fiberfill
- 4 buttons
- jute
- hot glue gun
- dried greenery with berries

Refer to Embroidery Stitches, page 135, and use 3 strands of floss for all stitching.

1. Use a stamp pad to ink the baby's hand; gently press onto muslin.

2. Write the child's name and the year on tracing paper to fit under handprint. Trace the holly design, page 138, on each side of the name.

3. Pin tracing paper design on muslin. Using the handprint and design as a guide, cut muslin into a square; cut a piece of batting the same size. Cut 2 squares from homespun 1¹/₄-inch larger than batting and muslin.

4. Center the batting, then the muslin on the right side of one homespun square. Using green floss, work Straight Stitches over the name, date and holly leaves, and Running Stitches along the outer edges of the muslin. Using red floss, work French Knots for the berries. Carefully tear away the tracing paper.

5. Using a ¹/₄-inch seam allowance, matching right sides and leaving an opening for stuffing, sew the homespun squares together. Turn right side out; stuff with fiberfill and sew the opening closed.

6. Sew a button to each front corner. For the hanger, knot the ends of a 14-inch length of jute around the top buttons. Glue greenery at the center of the hanger.

APPLIQUÉD FRAME

(shown on page 11)

- purchased photo mat (we used an 8"x10" mat with a 4¹/₂"x6¹/₂" opening)
- mat board
- homespun fabric for background
- cotton batting
- hot glue gun
- paper-backed fusible web
- assorted fabrics for appliqués
- photograph
- scrap of ribbon

1. Draw around the outer edge of the photo mat on a piece of mat board; cut out. Draw around the inner and outer edges of the photo mat on the wrong side of the background fabric. Cutting one inch from the drawn lines, cut out the fabric shape (**Fig. 1**); clip the inner corners to ¹/₈-inch from the drawn lines.

Fig. 1

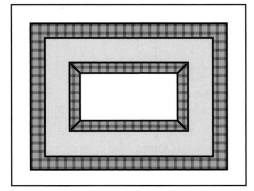

2. Using the mat as a pattern, cut out a piece of batting. Glue the batting to the mat. Center the mat batting side down on the wrong side of fabric. Fold the fabric edges at the opening of the mat to back; glue in place. Fold the corners of the fabric diagonally over the corners of the mat; glue in place. Fold the remaining fabric edges to the back of the mat; glue in place.

3. Using the patterns, page 139, follow *Making Appliqués*, page 134, to make 3 stars; 2 tree section C's; and one each of the reindeer, nose, tree section A, tree section B, small trunk and large trunk appliqués. Arrange and fuse the appliqués on the frame.

4. Center and glue the photo in the frame opening and the mat board to the back of the frame.

5. For the stand, cut a 1¹/₂-inch-wide piece of mat board the height of the frame. Bend the stand one inch from the top; glue the top section to the center top edge on the back of the frame. For stability, glue a length of ribbon between the frame and the stand.

DATED ORNAMENT

(shown on page 14)

- wooden frame (ours measures 5¹/₄"x6¹/₄")
- red spray paint
- 4 wooden stars
- yellow acrylic paint
- paintbrush
- black permanent fine-point pen
- card stock
- colored pencils
- cardboard for backing
- hot glue gun
- 20-inches of black craft wire
- greenery

1. Paint the frame red and stars yellow; let dry. Use the pen to write numbers for the year on the stars.

2. Photocopy snowman design, page 154, onto card stock. Color the design using colored pencils.

3. Center design in opening of frame and trim to fit. For the backing, cut a piece of cardboard the same size as the design. Glue the design and backing in the opening of the frame.

4. For the hanger, wrap wire around a pencil; remove the wire and bend into a "U" shape. Glue greenery and ends of the hanger to the top of the frame. Glue the stars to the hanger.

"DEAR SANTA" COOKIE PLATE

(shown on page 15)

- clear 9-inch dia. glass plate
- Delta Air Dry Perm Enamel™ Surface Cleaner and Conditioner
- tracing paper
- tape
- acrylic enamel gloss paint in desired colors
- small round paintbrushes
- Delta Air Dry Perm Enamel™ Clear Gloss Glaze

Follow manufacturer's instructions to apply conditioner, paint and glaze. Allow paint and glaze to dry after each application.

1. Wash and dry the plate. Use a paper towel to clean the back of the plate with surface cleaner and conditioner.

2. Trace Santa pattern, page 140, onto tracing paper. Tape the pattern to the front of the plate so that the design can be seen through the back.

3. Since you're painting on the back of the plate so the finished design will show through to the front, you need to start with the outlines, words and details like the dots on Santa's hat. When those have dried, paint the small areas of color like the cheeks, mouth, patches and stripes on Santa's hat. After those areas have dried, paint the large areas of color like the mustache, beard, face, hat and rim of the plate.

4. Apply 2 coats of glaze over the back of the plate. Follow manufacturer's instructions for curing paint and washing.

SPICED CANDLES

(shown on pages 16, 17 and 18)

- newspaper
- electric skillet
- wax
- old candles or crayons for color
- large coffee can
- craft sticks
- 2 jelly roll pans
- aluminum foil
- assorted spices (we used ground cinnamon, cloves and allspice)
- assorted taper and pillar candles

1. Cover your work area with newspaper.

2. Heat one inch of water to boiling in electric skillet.

3. Place wax and old candles or crayons in the coffee can; place the can in boiling water. Reduce heat to simmer. Stir with a craft stick until the wax is melted.

4. Line the jelly roll pans with aluminum foil.

5. Pour the spices in a thin layer on the bottom of one pan.

6. Pour just enough wax to cover the bottom of the remaining pan.

7. Covering the candle evenly, roll the candle in wax. Roll the candle in spices while wax is still warm. Repeat several times to create a nubby-textured candle; end with a coat of wax. Allow to harden.

8. To cover the top of the candle, use a craft stick to dab wax on the top of the candle. Sprinkle with spices.

STORYBOOK SANTA WALL HANGING

(shown on page 22)

- embroidery floss (see color key, page 142)
- #24 tapestry needle
- 13"x19" piece of Cream Cashel Linen® (28ct)
- Mill Hill Beads (#02013)
- beading needle
- 1/4-yard of red fabric
- 1/4-yard of green plaid fabric
- 7"x18" piece of fabric for hanging sleeve
- 19 1/2"x25 1/2" piece of muslin for backing
- 19"x25" piece of cotton batting
- craft saw
- 3/4-inch dia. wooden dowel
- craft glue
- two 7/8-inch dia. wooden buttons
- wood-tone spray
- one yard of 1/2-inch dia. green cord for hanger

Use a 1/4-inch seam allowance for all sewing unless otherwise indicated. Allow glue and wood-tone spray to dry after each application.

1. Following *Cross Stitch*, page 136, and using 3 strands of floss or blending filament for Cross Stitch and one strand for Backstitch, French Knots and to attach beads, work the Storybook Santa design, pages 142-143, over 2 fabric threads on linen. For the center section, trim the finished piece to 15 1/2"x9 1/2".

2. Cut two 11 1/2"x15 1/2" side inner borders and two 11 1/2"x11 1/2" top/bottom inner borders from red fabric. Cut two 4 1/2"x17 1/2" side outer borders and two 4 1/2"x19 1/2" top/bottom outer borders from green fabric.

3. Matching right sides and raw edges, sew the sides, then top and

bottom inner borders to the center section. Repeat to add the outer borders to complete the wall hanging front.

4. Press the short edges of the hanging sleeve ¼-inch to the wrong side; repeat and stitch in place. Matching wrong sides and raw edges, press the sleeve in half lengthwise.

5. Center raw edges of the hanging sleeve along top edge on the right side of the wall hanging front. Center right side of backing over hanging sleeve and wall hanging front. Center batting on wrong side of backing. Pin front, hanging sleeve, backing and batting together.

6. Leaving an opening at bottom for turning, sew together through all layers; clip the corners. Carefully turn the wall hanging right side out; stitch the opening closed. Stitch the bottom of the hanging sleeve to the backing, taking care not to stitch through to the front of the wall hanging.

7. Using the saw, cut a 22-inch length from dowel; glue a button to each end and spray with wood-tone spray. Insert the dowel through the hanging sleeve.

8. For the hanger, refer to **Figs. 1-3** to tie a knot at the center of the cord. Centering the knot above the wall hanging, knot the cord ends around the dowel and glue to secure; allow to dry, then trim the ends.

Fig. 1

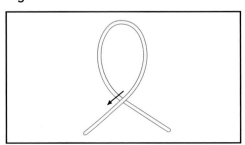

Fig. 2

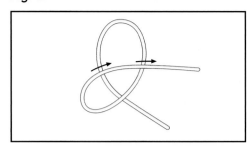

Fig. 3

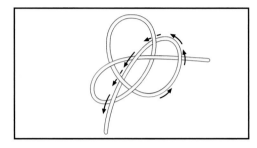

SNOWMAN BOWL

(shown on page 24)

- 4-inch dia. plastic foam ball
- instant papier-mâché
- wooden toothpick
- white and orange acrylic paint
- paintbrushes
- snow texturing medium
- brown permanent fine-point pen
- black rocks (we used aquarium gravel) for the eyes and mouth
- hot glue gun
- two 1½-inch dia. circles each of cardboard and batting
- two 2½-inch dia. fabric circles
- black chenille stem
- 11-inch dia. basket
- craft saw
- two 12-inch wooden spoons
- 3"x36" piece of fabric for scarf
- 16-inch fabric square for the liner

Allow papier-mâché, paint and snow texturing medium to dry after each application.

1. For the head, cover the foam ball with papier-mâché. Insert the toothpick halfway into the ball and form a carrot shape around the toothpick with papier-mâché.

2. Paint the head white; apply snow texturing medium to the entire head (except the nose). Paint the nose orange. Use the pen to draw detail lines on the nose.

3. Glue rocks to the head for the eyes and mouth.

4. For each earmuff, glue one batting circle to one cardboard circle. Center the circle batting side down on the wrong side of the fabric circle. Pulling taut, glue the raw edges of the fabric to the back of the cardboard. Cut a 6-inch length from the chenille stem; glue across the top of the head. Glue one earmuff piece to each side of the head, covering the ends of the chenille stem.

5. Cover the entire basket (except bottom) with papier-mâché.

6. For the arms, use a saw to cut 3½-inches from the handle of each spoon. Glue the spoons to the basket.

7. Paint the basket and arms white; cover with snow texturing medium.

8. Glue the head to the top edge of the basket.

9. Fringe the short edges of the scarf and tie around the neck.

10. Place the liner in the basket; fill with your favorite candy.

SNOWMAN ORNAMENTS

(shown on page 25)

- 4-inch dia. plastic foam ball
- instant papier-mâché
- wooden toothpick
- white and orange acrylic paint
- paintbrushes
- snow texturing medium
- brown permanent fine-point pen
- black rocks (we used aquarium gravel) for the eyes and mouth
- hot glue gun
- two 1½-inch dia. circles each of cardboard and batting
- two 2½-inch dia. fabric circles
- black chenille stem
- clear nylon thread

Allow papier-mâché, paint and snow texturing medium to dry after each application.

1. Follow Steps 1-4 of "Snowman Bowl," page 123, to make head.

2. For the hanger, thread a 7-inch length of nylon thread under the chenille stem; knot ends together.

SNOWBALLS

(described on page 25)

- assorted plastic foam balls
- instant papier-mâché
- snow texturing medium
- paintbrush
- glitter
- wax paper

1. Cover each foam ball with papier-mâché; allow to dry.

2. Apply snow texturing medium to each snowball. Sprinkle with glitter while the snow texturing medium is still wet. Allow snowballs to dry on wax paper.

GINGERBREAD WREATH

(shown on page 28)

- popcorn
- 24-inch dia. fresh evergreen wreath
- jute
- 3 Gingerbread Men cookies
- hot glue gun
- antique kitchen utensils
- 3"x22" strip of torn homespun
- floral wire

Make your gingerbread men using our recipe on page 77. Before you bake the cookies, use a straw to cut out a hole in the top for a hanger.

1. To make the garland, string the popcorn using a needle and thread; arrange on the wreath.

2. Thread a 14-inch length of jute through the hole in the top of each cookie; tie to the wreath.

3. Arrange and glue the utensils on the wreath.

4. Tie the strip of homespun into a bow. Wire the bow to the top of the wreath.

GINGERBREAD TREE

(shown on page 29)

- floral foam for fresh greenery
- 3-foot-tall fresh evergreen tree
- ceramic crock for tree stand
- Spanish moss
- popcorn
- jute
- Gingerbread Men cookies
- antique kitchen utensils
- hot glue gun
- dried apple and orange slices
- canella berries
- cinnamon sticks
- ½-yard of homespun fabric

Make your gingerbread men using our recipe on page 77. Before you bake the cookies, use a straw to cut out a hole in the top for a hanger.

1. Soak the foam in water. Place the tree in the crock; fill the area around the tree with foam to secure. Cover the foam with Spanish moss.

2. To make the garland, string the popcorn using a needle and thread; arrange on the tree as desired.

3. Thread a 14-inch length of jute through the hole in the top of each cookie; tie on the tree.

4. Arrange and glue utensils on the tree.

5. Arrange and glue orange slices, canella berries, apple slices and cinnamon sticks together to form clusters. Glue clusters on the tree.

6. Tie a 4"x22" strip of torn homespun into a bow around the top of the tree. Tear homespun into several 1¼"x22" strips; tie into bows and glue to the tree.

FELT ORNAMENTS

(shown on pages 36 and 37)

- paper-backed fusible web
- assorted colors of felt (we tea-dyed our white felt)
- pinking shears
- black felt for background
- black embroidery floss
- craft glue
- jingle bells
- assorted buttons
- black craft wire

Use pinking shears to cut out some of the shapes for added texture.

1. Using patterns, page 146, follow *Making Appliqués*, page 134, to make appliqués from felt for desired ornament.

2. Arrange and fuse shapes on black felt. Leaving a 1/4-inch black border, cut out ornament.

3. Using 3 strands of floss, work desired *Embroidery Stitches,* page 135, on ornament.

4. For the bell's bow, work Blanket Stitches along each long edge of a 3/4"x6" strip of felt. Overlap and glue the ends at center back. Wrap a 1/2"x1 1/4" strip of felt around the center of the bow; glue the ends at back to secure. For the streamers, cut two 3/4"x2" strips of felt; notch one end of each strip. Glue the streamers to the back of the bow; glue the bow to the ornament.

5. Embellish your work with jingle bells and buttons to make each ornament unique.

6. For the hanger, wrap a 10-inch length of wire around a pencil. Remove the wire from pencil and bend into a "U" shape; form a small loop at each end. Sew the loops to the back of the ornament.

LARGE TOPIARY
(shown on page 41)

- 6-inch high clay pot
- homespun fabrics
- hot glue gun
- floral foam
- plaster-of-paris
- 12-inch twigs or cinnamon sticks
- Spanish moss
- 12-inch-high foam cone
- pine cones
- acorns
- nuts
- assorted naturals
- raffia

1. Center pot on wrong side of fabric; tuck raw edges inside the pot and glue in place. Tie a strip of homespun around the pot.

2. Place small wedges of foam in the pot; fill with fairly thick mixture of plaster-of-paris. Place twigs or cinnamon sticks in the pot's center before the plaster hardens.

3. After the plaster hardens, cover with moss for a finished look.

4. Apply glue to end of twigs, insert twigs in bottom of cone. Glue assorted pine cones, acorns, nuts and other naturals to the cone. Embellish with raffia for garland.

FRAMED ANGEL
(shown on page 44)

- tea bag
- 6 1/2"x8 1/2" piece of torn muslin
- tracing paper
- gold, red, green, brown and black embroidery floss
- cardboard
- 10 1/2"x12 1/2" wooden frame (with a 7 1/2"x9 1/2" opening)
- 1/4-yard of fabric
- spray adhesive
- candle
- red acrylic paint
- paintbrush
- sandpaper
- wood glue
- kraft paper
- assorted rusty tin stars

Refer to Embroidery Stitches, page 135, and use 3 strands of floss for all stitching.

1. Refer to *Tea Dyeing,* page 134, to dye muslin.

2. Trace the angel pattern, page 147, onto tracing paper. Center and pin the design on muslin.

3. Referring to pattern for color placement, work French Knots for hair and eyes and Backstitches over the rest of the design; carefully remove the paper.

4. Cut a piece of cardboard to fit in the frame. Cut a piece of fabric one inch larger on all sides than the cardboard.

5. Center stitched design on the fabric piece; work Running Stitches along the edges. Spray the wrong side of fabric with spray adhesive; smooth onto cardboard piece, wrapping edges to the back.

6. Lightly drag the candle along the outer and inner edges of the frame, and on front of the frame.

7. Paint the frame red; let dry. Lightly sand the frame to give it a weathered look.

8. Glue the stitched piece in the frame.

9. Draw around the frame on kraft paper; cut out. Glue paper over the back of the frame.

10. Glue stars to the front of the frame.

ANGEL ORNAMENTS

(shown on page 45)

- tea bag
- tracing paper
- two 5"x9" pieces of muslin
- gold, red, green, brown and black embroidery floss
- batting
- polyester fiberfill
- buttons
- jute
- twigs for wings
- ivory acrylic paint
- paintbrush
- hot glue gun

Refer to Embroidery Stitches, page 135, and use 3 strands of floss for all stitching .

1. Follow Steps 1-3 of "Framed Angel," page 125, to stitch angel design (without wings and message) on one muslin piece.

2. Place the batting between the stitched design and second piece of muslin. Leaving an opening for stuffing, use black floss to work Running Stitches around the design.

3. Lightly stuff with fiberfill; stitch opening closed. Cut out. Stitching through all layers, sew buttons to the front of the angel.

4. For the hanger, knot the ends of a 5-inch length of jute together. Sew the knot to the back of the angel.

5. For the wings, paint the twigs ivory; let dry. Glue the twigs to the back of the angel.

SQUARE DOILY SACHET

(continued from page 50)

- tea bag
- one 5³/4-inch square doily
- one oval doily (ours measures 5¹/2"x9¹/2")
- embroidery floss
- ivory button
- potpourri

Refer to Embroidery Stitches, page 135, and use 6 strands of embroidery floss for all stitching.

1. Refer to *Tea Dyeing*, page 134, to dye doilies.

2. Using floss and knotting the ends at the front, sew the button to the center of the square doily.

3. With the oval doily extending at top for the flap and aligning fabric edges at bottom, pin the doilies wrong sides together. Work Running Stitches along the side and bottom edges of the square doily. Use Running Stitches to work the word "Noel" on the right side of the flap.

4. Lightly stuff the sachet with potpourri.

5. Fold the flap to the front of the sachet. Insert the button through the lace of the flap to secure.

SANTA STAR TREE TOPPER

(shown on page 52)

- tracing paper
- wool fabric (we used a striped wool blanket)
- ¹/4-yard of red fabric for backing
- 1³/8-inch dia. muslin circle for face
- black embroidery floss
- polyester fiberfill
- hot glue gun
- two ¹/8-inch dia. black beads
- natural wool roving
- scrap of ribbon
- miniature wooden toys, cutouts and ornaments
- artificial greenery
- jingle bells
- jute

1. Enlarging by 10%, photocopy the star top, middle and bottom patterns, page 150. Follow *Making Patterns*, page 134, to make a whole star pattern; cut out. Using the whole pattern and cutting ¹/4-inch outside the drawn line, cut one star each from wool and red fabric.

2. For the face, center the muslin circle on the top point of the wool star; stitch in place. Place the stars wrong sides together. Using 2 strands of floss and leaving an opening for stuffing, work *Running Stitches*, page 135, along the edges of the star.

3. Stuff the star with fiberfill and stitch the opening closed.

4. Glue beads to face for eyes. Glue wool roving around the face for the beard, hair and pom-pom on hat.

5. Tie ribbon into a bow. Arrange and glue the bow, miniature toys, cutouts and ornaments on the greenery; glue greenery to arm.

6. Sew a bell to each point of the star. Tie a length of jute into a bow around Santa's waist.

7. For the hanger, knot the ends of a 5-inch length of jute together. Sew the knot to the top back of Santa.

TREE SKIRT

(shown on page 53)

- 1½-yards of 60-inch-wide red wool fabric
- string
- chalk pencil
- thumbtack
- tea bags
- 2-yards of 60-inch wide white wool fabric
- tracing paper
- black heavy-duty thread
- fifty-five 9mm jingle bells

1. Matching right sides, fold the red fabric square in half from top to bottom and again from left to right.

2. Tie one end of string to a pencil. Insert a thumbtack through the string 2-inches from the pencil. Insert the thumbtack through the fabric as shown in **Fig. 1**; mark the inner cutting line.

Fig. 1

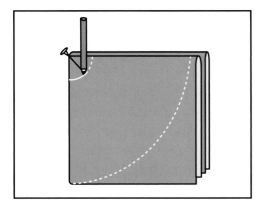

3. Repeat Step 2, inserting thumbtack 24½-inches from the pencil; mark the outside cutting line.

4. Cut along drawn lines through all fabric layers. For the opening in the back of the skirt, cut through one layer of fabric along one fold line from the outer to the inner edge.

5. Follow *Tea Dyeing*, page 134, to dye white fabric; allow to dry.

6. Using 2-inches for inner cutting line and 25-inches for outer cutting line, repeat Steps 1-4 to make the liner from dyed fabric.

7. Trace star and scallop patterns, page 151, onto tracing paper; cut out. Using the scallop pattern and beginning at one inside edge, mark scallops along the outer edge of the red fabric circle; cut along the drawn line.

8. Matching inner edges and back openings, place the liner under the red fabric. Using 2 strands of thread, work *Running Stitches*, page 135, along the scalloped edge to stitch together. Cut the liner fabric ½-inch from the scalloped edge of the red fabric.

9. Using the star pattern, cut 11 stars from remaining dyed fabric. Spacing evenly, pin stars around the skirt; work Running Stitches around the edges of each star to secure.

10. Sew jingle bells to the points of each star.

SPONGE-PAINTED GIFT WRAP

(shown on pages 56 and 57)

- tracing paper
- compressed craft sponge
- red, green and brown acrylic paint
- kraft paper
- assorted brown paper bags
- purchased natural card with envelope
- paintbrush
- spray adhesive
- checked tissue paper
- hot glue gun
- red buttons
- hole punch
- raffia
- greenery
- cinnamon sticks
- apple picks

Refer to Painting Techniques, page 134, for painting tips from your Country Friends® and allow paint to dry after each application.

1. Trace leaf and apple patterns, page 139, onto tracing paper; cut out. Using patterns, cut shapes from compressed sponge.

2. Use apple sponge and red paint to paint apples on kraft paper, bags and the front of the card; use leaf sponge and green paint to add the leaves. Paint a brown stem on each apple.

3. Use spray adhesive to attach strips of tissue paper to accent the card, envelope and bags as desired. Glue buttons to each tissue paper border.

4. To make a tag, cut a painted apple from kraft paper. Punch a hole in the top of the tag and attach to the package with raffia.

5. Embellish your packages with raffia bows, greenery, cinnamon sticks and apple picks.

HOLIDAY STATIONERY SETS
(shown on page 58)

FOLDER
- assorted colors of corrugated craft cardboard
- straight-edge craft scissors
- assorted colors of card stock
- craft glue
- hole punch
- decorative-edge craft scissors
- jute
- white flecked stationery paper
- colored pencils
- black permanent fine-point pen

Use straight-edge scissors for all cutting unless otherwise indicated. Allow glue to dry after each application.

1. For the cover, cut two 7"x9¹/2" pieces from cardboard. For pockets, cut two 4¹/2"x7" pieces from card stock. Leaving the top edge open, glue the edges of card stock to wrong side of each cardboard piece.

2. Matching pockets, place the front and back covers together; using the hole punch, punch 4 holes evenly along one edge.

3. For the spine, use craft scissors to cut a 2"x9¹/2" piece from card stock; fold in half lengthwise. Place the left edge of the cover into the fold; using the holes as a guide, punch holes in the spine. Thread a length of jute through each hole; tie into a bow at front to secure.

4. Enlarging the copy size by 10%, copy Santa or Snowman design, page 155, onto paper; color with colored pencils. Cut out design to measure 2⁷/8"x5". Use the pen to add detail lines along the edges.

5. Glue design to card stock; leaving a ¹/4-inch border, use craft scissors to cut out. Glue design to cardboard; leaving a ¹/4-inch border, cut out.

6. Cut a 1"x3" piece of paper. Use pen to write "Holiday Notes" on paper and draw detail lines around the edges. Glue the paper to card stock; leaving a ¹/4-inch border, use craft scissors to cut out. Glue the card stock to cardboard; leaving a ¹/4-inch border, cut out.

7. Arrange and glue design and message on front cover.

STATIONERY AND ENVELOPES
- eight 8¹/2"x11" sheets of white flecked stationery paper
- black permanent fine-point pen
- 16 white flecked envelopes
- colored pencils

Copies will make one set each of Santa and Snowman stationery.

1. Copy stationery designs, page 155, onto paper; cut in half.

2. Use pen to draw swirls or stars along the edge of flap on envelope.

3. Color the designs and envelopes with colored pencils.

ADDRESS BOOK
- white flecked stationery paper
- colored pencils
- decorative-edge craft scissors
- craft glue
- green card stock
- natural craft cardboard
- hole punch
- red embroidery floss

Use straight-edge scissors for all cutting unless otherwise indicated. Allow glue to dry after each application.

1. Copy Santa or snowman design, page 155, onto paper; color with colored pencils. With design near bottom, use craft scissors to cut out design to measure 3"x3³/4". Glue the design to green card stock; leaving a ¹/8-inch border, cut out.

2. For the cover, cut a 5"x8¹/2" piece of cardboard. Matching short edges and wrong sides, fold cover in half. For the pages, cut ten 4"x4³/4" pieces from paper. Use craft scissors to trim ¹/4-inch from one long edge on each piece of paper. Matching decorative edges, stack pages. Place straight edge of pages in fold of cover.

3. Using the hole punch, evenly punch 4 holes along the spine of book. Using 6 strands of floss, sew the book together by stitching through the holes and around the spine; knot ends at back.

4. Glue design to front of cover and buttons to each corner.

CHRISTMAS TREE COVERLET
(continued from page 60)

♥Rnd 5: With **right** side facing, join Dark Spruce with slip st in any corner ch-1 sp; ch 4, (dc in same sp, ch 1) 4 times, skip next dc, (dc in next dc, ch 1, skip next dc) across to next ch-1 sp, ★ (dc, ch 1) 5 times in ch-1 sp, skip next dc, (dc in next dc, ch 1, skip next dc) across to next ch-1 sp; repeat from ★ around; join with slip st to third ch of beginning ch-4, finish off.

ASSEMBLY
♥Place two Strips with **wrong** sides together and bottom edges at same end. With Dark Spruce and working through **inside** loops of each stitch on **both** pieces, whip stitch Strips together, beginning in first corner dc and ending in next corner dc. Repeat to add the remaining Strips.

EDGING
♥Rnd 1: With **right** side facing, join Dark Spruce with sc in any st; sc evenly around entire Afghan working 3 sc in each corner dc; join with slip st to first sc.

♥**Rnd 2:** Ch 1, working from **left** to **right**, work reverse sc in each sc around; join with slip st to first st, finish off.

♥With Burgundy and using photo as a guide for placement, add bows to tops of trees.

CARDINAL MITTENS

(shown on page 66)

- tracing paper
- assorted colors of felt
- pair of fleece mittens
- black embroidery floss
- two 3/8-inch dia. buttons

Refer to Embroidery Stitches, page 135, and use 3 strands of floss for all stitching.

1. Trace patterns, page 156, onto tracing paper; cut out.

2. Using the patterns, cut 2 of each shape from felt.

3. Pin the branch to one mitten front; work a Blanket Stitch around the edges of the branch to secure. Arrange the cardinal body, beak and face on the branch; pin in place. Work Blanket Stitches along edges of appliqués.

4. Center the leaves below the cardinal; sew a button to the middle of the leaves to secure.

5. Reversing all felt shapes, repeat Steps 3-4 to embellish the remaining mitten.

SNOWMAN PIN

(continued from page 67)

7. Paint one end of toothpick orange; allow to dry. Cut 3/4-inch from painted end of toothpick. Glue nose and twigs in holes.

8. For the scarf, tie a torn strip of fabric around snowman's neck.

9. Glue button and greenery to the cuff of the hat. Glue the pin back to the back of the snowman.

FAMILY TOBOGGANS

(shown on page 68)

ABBREVIATIONS

K	Knit
mm	millimeters
P	purl
PSSO	pass slipped stitch over
st(s)	stitches
tog	together

★ - work instructions following ★ as many **more** times as indicated in addition to the first time.

( ) or [ ] - work enclosed instructions **as many** times as specified by the number immediately following **or** work all enclosed instructions in the stitch or space indicated **or** contains explanatory remarks.

SIZE (HEAD MEASUREMENT):

Child

2-4 (16½") 6-8 (18") 10-12 (19½")

Adult

7 (21")   8 (22½")   9 (24")

Size Note: Instructions are written for Children's sizes in first braces { } with Adult sizes in second braces { }. Instructions will be easier to read if you circle all the numbers pertaining to your size.

MATERIALS

Worsted Weight Yarn:
(3½-3½-4)(4-4½-4½) ounces, [(100-100-110)(110-130-130) grams, (200-200-225) (225-255-255) yards]
Straight knitting needles, sizes 5 (3.75 mm) **and** 7 (4.50 mm) **or** sizes needed for gauge
Markers
Yarn needle

GAUGE: With larger size needles, in Stockinette Stitch, 20 sts and 28 rows = 4"

For striped Cap, change colors every 2 rows in Body.

RIBBING

With smaller size needles, cast on {78-84-90}{102-108-114} sts **very loosely**.

Work in K1, P1 ribbing for {1-1-1}{1½-1½-1½}".

BODY

Change to larger size needles. Work in Stockinette Stitch until Cap measures {3½-4-4½}{5-5½-6}" from cast on edge, ending by working a **purl** row.

TOP SHAPING

Row 1 (Decrease row):
K {10-11-12}{14-15-16}, slip 1 as if to **knit**, K2 tog, PSSO, ★ place marker, K {10-11-12}{14-15-16}, slip 1 as if to **knit**, K2 tog, PSSO; repeat from ★ across: {66-72-78}{90-96-102} sts.

Row 2: Purl across.

Row 3 (Decrease row): Knit across to within 3 sts of next marker, slip 1 as if to **knit**, K2 tog, PSSO, ★ slip marker, knit across to within 3 sts of next marker, slip 1 as if to **knit**, K2 tog, PSSO; repeat from ★ across: {54-60-66}{78-84-90} sts.

Row 4: Purl across.
Repeat Rows 3 and 4, {4-4-5}{6-6-7} times: {6-12-6}{6-12-6} sts.

Cut yarn, leaving a 20-inch end. Thread yarn needle with end and weave through remaining sts, pulling firmly to close; sew seam (**Fig. 1**). Add pom-pom.

Fig. 1

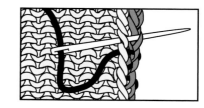

CHRISTMAS CARDIGAN
(shown on page 69)

- sweatshirt with set-in sleeves
- 3"x90" strip of fabric for binding (pieced as necessary)
- two ³/₄-inch dia. buttons
- 5³/₄"x6³/₄" piece of fusible interfacing for pocket
- 7³/₄"x9³/₄" piece of fabric for pocket
- black permanent fine-point pen
- 2¹/₄"x4³/₄" piece of fabric for sign
- assorted buttons
- embroidery floss
- paper-backed fusible web
- assorted fabrics for appliqués
- ¹/₄-yard of ¹/₄-inch-wide grosgrain ribbon

Refer to Embroidery Stitches, page 135, and use 3 strands of floss for all stitching.

1. Remove cuffs and bottom band from sweatshirt. Using a yardstick, draw a line down the center front of the sweatshirt; cut sweatshirt open along the line.

2. Matching wrong sides and long edges, press the binding strip in half; unfold. Matching wrong sides, press each long raw edge to the center fold; refold strip.

3. For each sleeve, measure around the bottom edge of sleeve; add ¹/₂-inch. Cut a strip of binding the determined measurement; press one end ¹/₄-inch to the wrong side. Beginning with the unpressed end, insert edge of sleeve into fold of strip; top stitch in place.

4. For cuff on each sleeve, make a one inch pleat in sleeve (**Fig. 1**). Sewing through all layers, tack a ³/₄-inch dia. button over pleat to secure.

Fig. 1

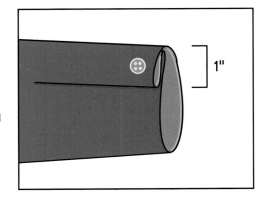

5. Measure along bottom edge of sweatshirt. Cut a piece of binding the determined measurement. Insert bottom edge into fold of binding; top stitch in place.

6. For each front edge, measure along edge; add ¹/₂-inch. Cut a piece of binding the determined measurement. Press each end ¹/₄-inch to the wrong side. Insert edge into fold of binding; top stitch in place.

7. Center and fuse interfacing on wrong side of pocket fabric. Press the side and bottom edges of pocket one inch to the wrong side. Press the top edge 1¹/₂-inches to the wrong side.

8. Leaving a space for the button "O" between the letters "N" and "E," use the pen to write "NOEL" on the sign. Fringe the edges of the sign ¹/₄-inch. Sew a button to the sign to complete the word "NOEL."

9. Center the sign on the pocket ¹/₂-inch from the top edge. Work Running Stitches along the edges of the sign.

10. Pin pocket to cardigan. Top stitch along the side and bottom edges.

11. Using patterns, page 148, follow *Making Appliqués*, page 134, to make 2 each (one in reverse) of star, gingerbread man, stocking, cuff and heart appliqués. Arrange all appliqués except cuffs on cardigan; fuse in place. For each stocking hanger, fold a 3¹/₄-inch length of ribbon in half. Place the ends under the cuff pieces and fuse in place.

12. Work Blanket Stitches along the edges of each appliqué and French Knots for the eyes on the gingerbread men. Embellish your appliqués with buttons and bows.

YULETIDE JARS
(shown on pages 72 and 73)

- assorted small jars with lids
- kraft paper
- decorative-edge craft scissors
- rubber band
- jute
- assorted buttons
- card stock for photocopies of tags and labels
- colored pencils
- craft glue
- scraps of homespun
- pinking shears
- black permanent fine-point pen
- hot glue gun
- scrap of batting
- hole punch
- raffia

Use craft glue for all gluing unless otherwise indicated; allow to dry after each application.

GOOD TIDINGS JAR

1. Draw around jar lid on kraft paper; use craft scissors to cut out 1¹/₂-inches outside the drawn line.

2. Center the circle on the lid and secure with a rubber band. Wrap a length of jute around the lid; thread the ends through a button and tie into a bow.

3. Using design, page 154, follow *Making a Tag or Label*, page 134, to make label; center and glue to top of the lid.

HEART 'N HOMESPUN JAR

1. Draw around the jar lid on wrong side of homespun; use pinking shears to cut out 1¹/2-inches outside the drawn line.

2. Remove the band from the jar; center the circle over the lid and replace the band.

3. Draw a heart on kraft paper; cut out. Use the pen to write message on the label and draw "stitches" around the edge; glue to front of the jar.

4. Tie a length of jute into a bow around the lid. Hot glue a button to the center of the bow.

VEGETABLE JAR

1. Using design, page 154, follow *Making a Tag or Label*, page 134, to make label. Glue to the front of the jar.

2. Tie a strip of torn homespun around the lid.

KITCHEN ANGEL JAR

1. Draw around the lid on wrong side of homespun; cut out. Cut a piece of batting the same size.

2. Remove the band from the jar; center the batting, then the homespun over the lid and replace the band.

3. Using design, page 154, follow *Making a Tag or Label*, page 134, to make tag; punch a hole in corner.

4. Tie a length of raffia into a bow around jar. Use a length of raffia to tie tag to bow.

SANTA JAR

(shown on page 75)

- jar with lid (we used a one-quart mayonnaise jar)
- alcohol
- ivory enamel paint
- paintbrush
- yellow paint pen
- flesh and green felt
- spray adhesive
- craft glue
- 2¹/2-inch dia. plastic foam ball
- hot glue gun
- cotton batting
- rubber band
- toddler-size red sock
- green, gold and black embroidery floss
- small jingle bell
- tracing paper
- red candy

Allow paint and glue to dry after each application. Use craft glue for all gluing unless otherwise indicated.

1. Wipe the outside of the jar with alcohol; allow to dry. Paint a one inch wide ivory strip down the jar and around the bottom for the coat trim. Use the paint pen to draw snowflakes on the trim.

2. Draw around the jar lid on green felt; cut out ¹/2-inch outside the drawn line. Make clips in the edge to ¹/8-inch from drawn line. Apply spray adhesive to wrong side of circle. Center the flat side of the lid on the circle and smooth in place; smooth the clipped edges over the edge. Place the lid on the jar. Measure around the lid and add ¹/2-inch; measure the height of the lid. Cut a strip of green felt the determined measurements. Overlapping ends at back, glue strip around lid.

3. For the head, flatten the bottom of the foam ball; hot glue to the center of the lid. Overlapping the ends at back, wrap a 4¹/2"x9¹/2" piece of batting around the head; glue the short ends to secure. Gather the batting at the top of the head and secure with a rubber band. For the hat, arrange the sock on the head over the gathers; glue to secure. Use green floss to tie the bell to the tip of the hat.

4. For the hat cuff, measure around the bottom edge of the hat; add ¹/2-inch. Cut a piece of batting 3-inches wide by the determined measurement. Fold the long edges under ³/4-inch; glue in place. Using 6 strands of floss, work *Straight Stitches*, page 135, for stars along the center of the cuff. Overlapping ends at back, wrap the cuff around the bottom edge of the hat; glue in place.

5. Trace the patterns, page 156, onto tracing paper; cut out. Using the patterns, cut mustache and beard from batting and face from flesh-colored felt. Make 2-inch cuts in the bottom of the beard for whiskers.

6. For the eyes, use 3 strands of black floss to make *French Knots*, page 135, on the face. Position and glue the face, beard and then the mustache on the head.

7. Fill the jar with your favorite red Christmas candy to give Santa his traditional red coat.

FENCE POST SANTA JAR

(shown on page 75)

- jumbo craft sticks
- rubber band
- jar with lid
- tracing paper
- transfer paper
- utility scissors
- acrylic paint in desired colors
- paintbrushes
- black permanent fine-point pen
- hot glue gun
- toothbrush
- white acrylic paint
- clear acrylic spray sealer
- candy
- fabric
- fiberfill
- jute

Refer to Painting Techniques, page 134, for painting tips from your Country Friends® and allow paint, glue and sealer to dry after each application.

1. To determine the number of craft sticks you'll need, use a rubber band to hold the sticks around jar.

2. Trace desired Santa patterns, page 156, onto tracing paper. Transfer the patterns onto craft sticks. Use utility scissors to cut off the bottom of each craft stick.

3. Paint the Santas; use the pen to add details.

4. Arrange and glue the Santas around the jar. Spatter paint the jar with white paint. Spray a coat of sealer over the entire jar.

5. Fill the jar with Christmas candy. Using a pencil, draw around lid on wrong side of fabric; cut out 3-inches outside the drawn line. Glue a small amount of fiberfill to the jar lid. Center the fabric circle over the lid and secure with a length of jute.

BREAD CLOTH

(shown on page 77)

- ³/4-yard of unbleached muslin
- assorted fabrics (we used ¹/8-yard for binding and scraps for appliqués)
- embroidery floss
- tracing paper
- paper-backed fusible web

Refer to Embroidery Stitches, page 135, and use 3 strands of floss for all stitching.

1. Cut a 22-inch square from muslin.

2. For the binding, cut a 2"x90" strip of fabric, piecing as necessary. Press one end ¹/4-inch to the wrong side. Matching wrong sides, press the strip in half lengthwise; unfold. Press each long raw edge to the center fold; refold the strip. Beginning with the unpressed end and mitering each corner, insert the edges of the bread cloth into the fold of the binding; pin in place. Using floss, work Running Stitches to sew the binding in place.

3. Trace the bread cloth design, page 157, onto tracing paper. Pin the pattern to one corner of the muslin square.

4. Referring to pattern for color suggestions and using desired stitches, stitch the design through tracing paper. When finished, carefully tear away the tracing paper.

5. Using the patterns, page 157, follow *Making Appliqués*, page 134, to make one heart A, 2 heart B and 2 gingerbread man appliqués. Arrange and fuse the appliqués in place. Work desired stitches over edges of appliqués to finish.

HOMESPUN GIFT BAG

(shown on page 78)

- paper-backed fusible web
- homespun fabric
- brown paper bag with handles (we used an 8"x10¹/2" bag)
- raffia
- hot glue gun
- button
- card stock
- corrugated craft cardboard
- hole punch

1. Cut a piece of web and fabric one inch smaller than the front of the bag. Fuse the fabric to the web, then to the front of the bag.

2. Tie several lengths of raffia into a bow. Glue the bow to the bag and the button to the knot of the bow.

3. Photocopy the tag design, page 154, onto card stock; cut out.

4. Glue the tag to cardboard. Leaving a ¹/4-inch border, cut out the tag.

5. Punch a hole in the corner of the tag. Use a length of raffia to tie the tag around the button.

FABRIC BAGS

(shown on page 81)

- assorted homespun fabrics
- paper-backed fusible web
- assorted colors of felt for appliqués
- embroidery floss
- muslin
- fabric glue
- miniature rusty tin stars
- jute

Refer to Embroidery Stitches, page 135, and use 2 strands of floss for all stitching.

1. For each bag, cut two 7"x9" pieces of fabric. Press one short edge of each piece 3/8-inch to the wrong side twice; sew in place. Matching right sides and hemmed edges and using a 1/4-inch seam allowance, sew along the side and bottom edges; turn the bag right side out.

2. Using desired patterns, page 143, follow *Making Appliqués*, page 134, to make appliqués from felt. Arrange appliqués on a 2"x21/2" piece of felt and fuse in place.

3. Embellish your design with Straight Stitches for the hair and French Knots for the eyes and snow.

4. Tear a 3"x31/2" piece of muslin. Center felt design on muslin; position muslin on bag. Use floss to work Blanket Stitches or Running Stitches along the edges of the felt background to secure muslin and felt design to bag.

5. Glue a tin star on design as desired.

6. Place a gift in the bag and tie closed with a length of jute.

BREAD BASKET

(shown on page 82)

- hot glue gun
- crocheted lace
- round wicker basket (we used an 11-inch dia. by 4-inch-high basket with handles)
- artificial greenery
- yellow acrylic paint
- paintbrush
- one large and 2 small wooden stars
- black permanent fine-point pen
- jute rope
- 24"x24" piece of fabric for liner

1. Overlapping the ends at back, glue lace around the basket just below the rim. Glue greenery to the front of the basket.

2. Paint the wooden stars yellow; let dry. Use the pen to write message and make dots on the large star. Glue the large star to the front of the basket.

3. Tie a length of jute around a loaf of bread; glue one small star to each end of jute. Place the fabric, bread and other goodies in the basket.

PIE TAG

(shown on page 85)

- card stock
- colored pencils
- decorative-edge craft scissors

1. Photocopy tag design, page 153, onto card stock.

2. Use pencils to color the tag design.

3. Use craft scissors to cut out the tag.

CHRISTMAS BOOKMARKS

(shown on page 64)

- assorted colors of card stock
- decorative-edge craft scissors
- straight-edge scissors
- black permanent fine-point pen
- colored pencils
- glue stick
- wrapping paper
- hot glue gun
- assorted buttons
- raffia

Use decorative-edge or straight-edge scissors as desired for all cutting.

1. Photocopy desired design, page 153, onto card stock; cut out. Use pen and colored pencils to color the design.

2. Use the glue stick to glue bookmark to a piece of wrapping paper or card stock. Leaving a border, cut out bookmark. Hot glue buttons to the corners of the bookmark.

3. Leaving 10-inch streamers, tie raffia into a bow. With bow extending 3/4-inch above the bookmark, hot glue streamers of bow to the back of the bookmark. Use glue stick to glue bookmark to a third piece of wrapping paper or card stock. Leaving a border, cut out the bookmark.

133

GENERAL INSTRUCTIONS

MAKING PATTERNS

When the entire pattern is shown, place tracing paper over the pattern and draw over lines. For a more durable pattern, use a permanent marker to draw over pattern on stencil plastic.

When patterns are stacked or overlapped, place tracing paper over the pattern and follow a single colored line to trace the pattern. Repeat to trace each pattern separately onto tracing paper.

When tracing a two-part pattern, match the dashed lines and arrows to trace the pattern onto tracing paper.

When only half of the pattern is shown (indicated by a solid blue line on pattern), fold the tracing paper in half. Place the fold along the blue line and trace pattern half; turn folded paper over and draw over the traced lines on the remaining side. Unfold the pattern; cut out.

MAKING APPLIQUÉS

To prevent darker fabrics from showing through, white or light-colored fabrics may need to be lined with fusible interfacing before being fused.

To make reverse appliqués, trace the pattern onto tracing paper; turn traced pattern over and continue to follow all steps using the reversed pattern.

1. Trace the appliqué pattern onto paper side of web as many times as indicated for a single fabric. When making more than one appliqué, leave at least one inch between shapes.

2. Cutting ½-inch outside the drawn shape, cut out the web shape. Fuse to the wrong side of the fabric.

3. Cut out the appliqué shape along the drawn lines.

PAINTING TECHNIQUES

Transferring a pattern: Trace pattern onto tracing paper. Place transfer paper coated side down between project and traced pattern. Use removable tape to secure pattern to project. Use a pencil to draw over outlines of design (press lightly to avoid smudges and heavy lines that are difficult to cover). If necessary, use a soft eraser to remove any smudges.

Painting base coats: Use a medium round brush for large areas and a small round brush for small areas. Do not overload brush. Allowing to dry between coats, apply several thin coats of paint to project.

Transferring details: To transfer detail lines to design, reposition pattern and transfer paper over painted base coats and use a pencil to lightly draw over detail lines of design.

Adding details: Use a permanent pen to draw over detail lines.

Sponge Painting: Place project on a covered work surface. Practice sponge-painting technique on scrap paper until desired look is achieved. Paint projects with first color and allow to dry before moving to next color. Use a clean sponge for each additional color.

For allover designs, dip a dampened sponge piece into paint; remove excess paint on a paper towel. Use a light stamping motion to paint item.

For painting with sponge shapes, dip a dampened sponge shape into paint; remove excess paint on a paper towel. Lightly press sponge shape onto project. Carefully lift sponge. For a reverse design, turn sponge shape over.

Sealing: If an item will be handled frequently or used outdoors, we recommend sealing the item with clear acrylic sealer. Sealers are available in spray or brush-on form in several finishes. Follow the manufacturer's instructions to apply the sealer.

Spatter Painting: Dip the bristle tips of a dry toothbrush into paint, blot on a paper towel to remove excess, then pull thumb across bristles to spatter paint on project.

TEA DYEING

1. Steep one tea bag in 2 cups of hot water; allow to cool.

2. Immerse fabric or lace into tea. Soak until desired color is achieved. Remove from tea and allow to dry. Press if desired.

MAKING A TAG OR LABEL

For a quick and easy tag or label, photocopy desired tag or label design and color with colored pencils or markers. Use straight-edge or decorative-edge craft scissors to cut out tag or label. Glue tag to colored paper or cardstock. Leaving a border around tag, cut tag from colored paper. Use pen or marker to write message on tag.

EMBROIDERY STITCHES

Preparing the floss: If your project will be laundered, soak floss in a mixture of one cup water and one tablespoon vinegar for a few minutes and allow to dry before using to prevent colors from bleeding or fading.

Backstitch: Referring to **Fig. 1**, bring needle up at 1; go down at 2; bring up at 3 and pull through. For next stitch, insert needle at 1; bring up at 4 and pull through.

Fig. 1

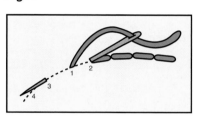

Blanket Stitch: Referring to **Fig. 2a**, bring needle up at 1. Keeping thread below point of needle, go down at 2 and come up at 3. Continue working as shown in **Fig. 2b**.

Fig. 2a

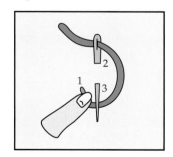

Fig. 2b

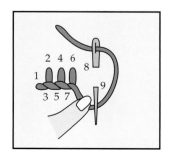

Cross Stitch: Referring to **Fig. 3**, bring needle up at 1; go down at 2. Bring needle up at 3; go down at 4. Repeat for each stitch.

Fig. 3

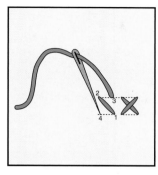

Feather Stitch: Bring needle up at 1 and down at 2, forming a "U" shape. Bring needle up at 3 inside stitch formed and then down at 4, forming another "U" (**Fig. 4**). End Feather Stitches by bringing needle up through last loop and straight down outside of loop.

Fig. 4

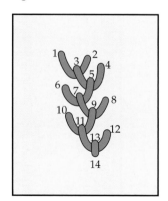

French Knot: Referring to **Fig. 5**, bring needle up at 1. Wrap floss once around needle and insert needle at 2, holding end of floss with non-stitching fingers. Tighten knot, then pull needle through fabric, holding floss until it must be released. For a larger knot, use more strands; wrap only once.

Fig. 5

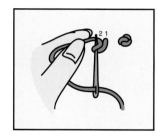

Running Stitch: Referring to **Fig. 6**, make a series of straight stitches with stitch length equal to the space between stitches.

Fig. 6

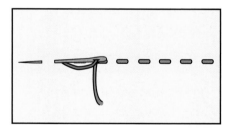

Straight Stitch: Referring to **Fig. 7**, come up at 1 and go down at 2.

Fig. 7

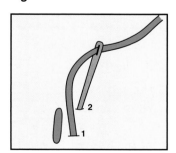

CROSS STITCH

Preparing the floss: If your project will be laundered, soak floss in a mixture of one cup water and one tablespoon vinegar for a few minutes and allow to dry before using to prevent colors from bleeding or fading.

Attaching beads: Refer to the chart for bead placement and sew bead in place using a fine needle that will pass through the bead. Bring the needle up at 1, run the needle through the bead and then down at 2. Secure the floss on the back or move to the next bead as shown in **Fig. 1**.

Fig. 1.

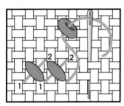

Counted Cross Stitch (X): Work one Cross Stitch to correspond to each colored square in chart. For horizontal rows, work stitches in two journeys.

Fig. 2

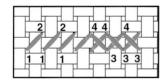

For vertical rows, complete stitch as shown.

Fig. 3

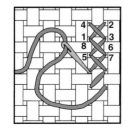

When working over 2 fabric threads, work Cross Stitch as shown.

Fig. 4

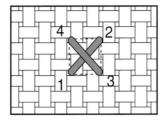

Quarter Stitch (¼ X): Quarter Stitches are shown by triangular shapes of color in chart and color key.

Fig. 5

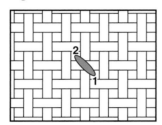

Backstitch (B'ST): For outline detail, Backstitch (shown in chart and color key by black or colored straight lines) should be worked after all Cross Stitch has been completed.

Fig. 6

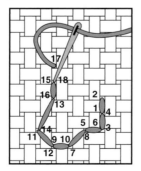

CROCHET
ABBREVIATIONS

ch(s)	chain(s)
dc	double crochet(s)
dtr	double treble crochet(s)
hdc	half double crochet(s)
mm	millimeters
Rnd(s)	Round(s)
sc	single crochet(s)
sp(s)	space(s)
st(s)	stitch(es)
tr	treble crochet(s)
YO	yarn over

★ - work instructions following ★ as many **more** times as indicated in addition to the first time.

† to † - work all instructions from first † to second † **as many** times as specified.

( ) or [ ] - work enclosed instructions **as many** times as specified by the number immediately following **or** work all enclosed instructions in the stitch **or** space indicated **or** contains explanatory remarks.

colon (:) - the number(s) given after a colon at the end of a row or round denote(s) the number of stitches you should have on that row or round.

Slip stitch (slip st): Insert hook in st or sp indicated, YO and draw through st or sp **and** through loop on hook (**Fig. 1**). To join with a slip st, begin with a slip knot on hook, insert hook in st or sp indicated, YO and draw through st or sp **and** through the slip knot on hook.

Fig. 1

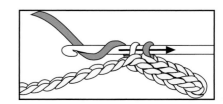

Single crochet (sc): Insert hook in st or sp indicated, YO and pull up a loop, YO and draw through both loops on hook (**Fig. 2**).

Fig. 2

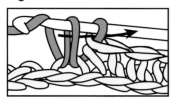

Half double crochet (hdc): YO, insert hook in st or sp indicated, YO and pull up a loop, YO and draw through all 3 loops on hook (**Fig. 3**).

Fig. 3

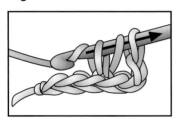

Double crochet (dc): YO, insert hook in st or sp indicated, YO and pull up a loop (3 loops on hook), YO and draw through 2 loops on hook (**Fig. 4a**), YO and draw through remaining 2 loops on hook (**Fig. 4b**).

Fig. 4a

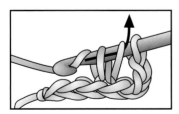

Fig. 4b

Treble crochet (tr): YO twice, insert hook in st or sp indicated, YO and pull up a loop (4 loops on a hook, **Fig. 5a**), (YO and draw through 2 loops on hook) 3 times (**Fig. 5b**).

Fig. 5a

Fig. 5b

Double treble crochet (dtr): YO 3 times, insert hook in st **or** sp indicated, YO and pull up a loop (5 loops on hook, **Fig. 6a**), (YO and draw through 2 loops on hook) 4 times (**Fig. 6b**).

Fig. 6a

Fig. 6b

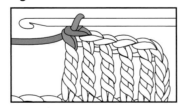

Free loops of a chain: When instructed to work in free loop of a chain, work in loop indicated by arrow (**Fig. 7**).

Fig. 7

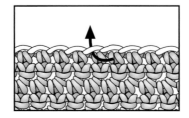

Changing colors: Work last sc before color change to last step (2 loops on hook), with new color, YO and draw through; drop old color (**Fig. 8**).

Fig. 8

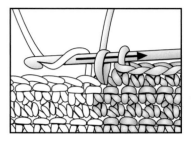

Reverse sc: Working from **left** to **right**, insert hook in st or sp to right of hook (**Fig. 9a**), YO and draw through, under and to left of loop on hook (2 loops on hook, **Fig. 9b**), YO and draw through both loops on hook (**Fig. 9c**) (reverse sc made, **Fig. 9d**).

Fig. 9a

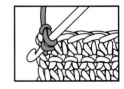

Fig. 9b

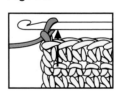

Fig. 9c

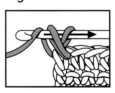

Fig. 9d

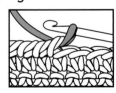

Finishing hints: Good finishing techniques make a big difference in the quality of the finished piece. Make a habit of weaving in loose ends as you work. To keep loose ends from showing, always weave them back through several stitches or work over them. When ends are secure, clip them off close to your work.

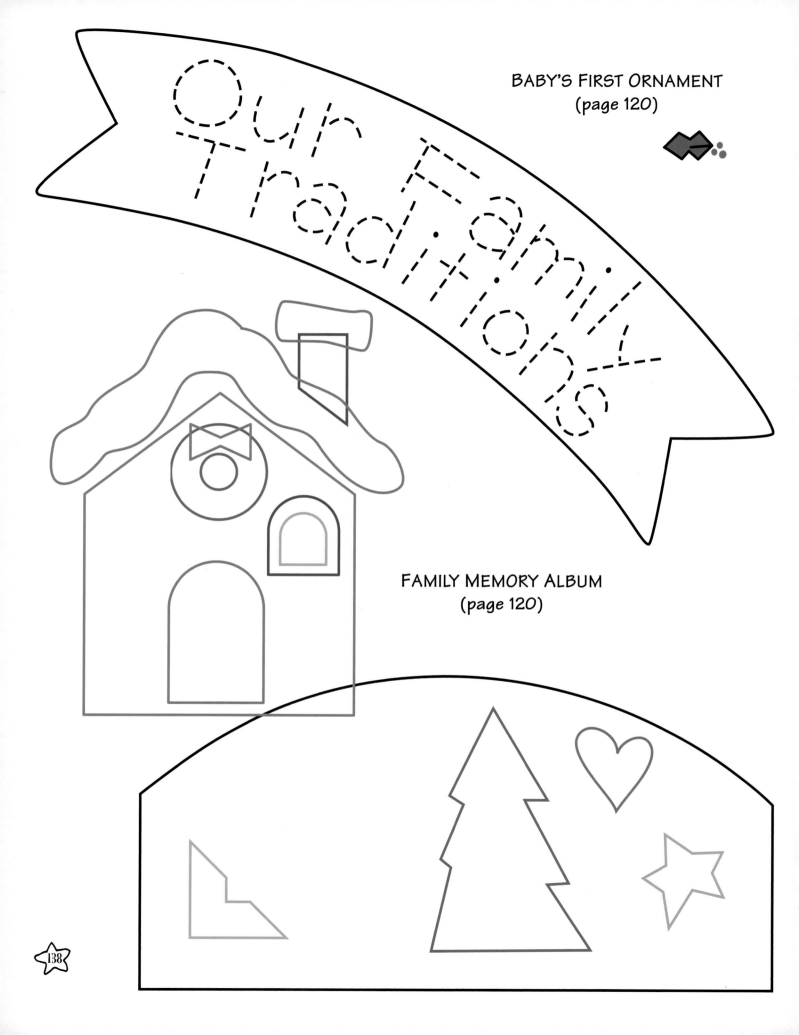

Our Family Traditions

BABY'S FIRST ORNAMENT
(page 120)

FAMILY MEMORY ALBUM
(page 120)

138

SPONGE-PAINTED
GIFT WRAP
(page 127)

HOMEMADE HOLIDAY
HAND TOWEL
(page 65)

APPLIQUÉD FRAME
(page 121)

A

B

C

SNOWMAN PILLOW
(page 26)

TEA TOWELS
(page 31)

N EL

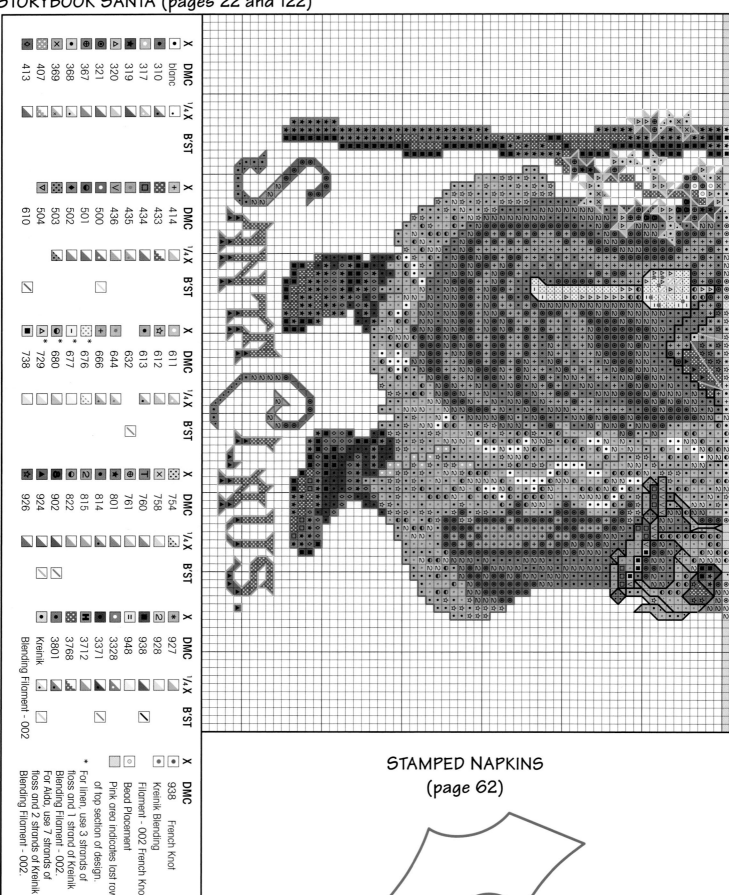

Color key (X / DMC / ¼X / B'ST):

DMC
blanc
310
317
319
320
321
367
368
369
407
413

DMC
414
433
434
435
436
500
501
502
503
504
610

DMC
611
612
613
632
644
666
676
677
680
729
738

DMC
754
758
760
761
801
814
815
822
902
924
926

DMC
927
928
938
948
3328
3371
3712
3768
3801
Kreinik Blending Filament - 002

X	DMC	
	938	French Knot
		Kreinik Blending Filament - 002 French Knot
		Bead Placement

Pink area indicates last row of top section of design.

* For linen, use 3 strands of floss and 1 strand of Kreinik Blending Filament - 002.
For Aida, use 7 strands of floss and 2 strands of Kreinik Blending Filament - 002.

STAMPED NAPKINS
(page 62)

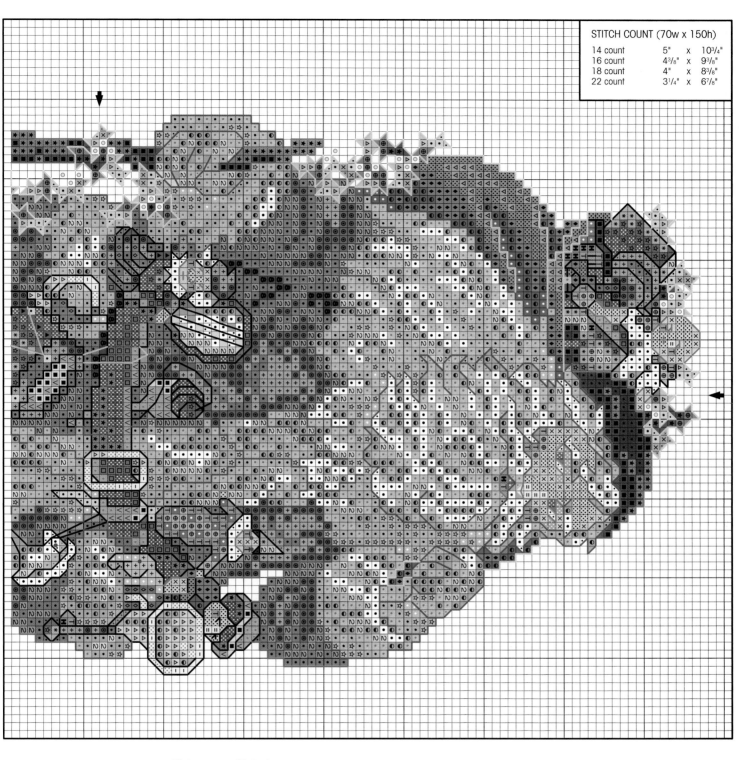

STITCH COUNT (70w x 150h)

14 count	5"	x	10³/₄"
16 count	4³/₈"	x	9³/₈"
18 count	4"	x	8³/₈"
22 count	3¹/₄"	x	6⁷/₈"

FABRIC BAGS
(page 133)

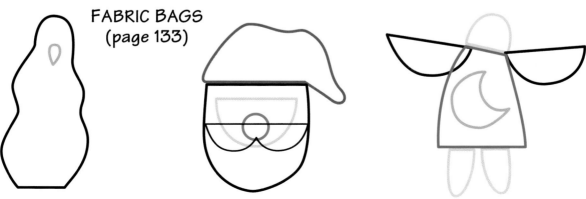

oh christmas tree

PRIMITIVE STOCKINGS
(page 34)

WArM NOÉL to YoU

STOCKING TOP

ANGELS WATCH
OVER thEE

STOCKING BOTTOM

FELT ORNAMENTS
(page 124)

Peace to All

FRAMED ANGEL &
ORNAMENTS
(pages 125 and 126)

MITTEN GARLAND
(page 47)

CHRISTMAS CARDIGAN
(page 130)

FLOOR CLOTH
(pages 48 and 49)

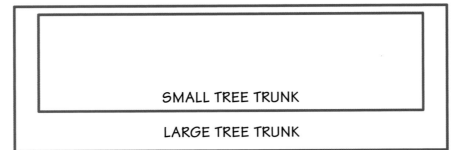

SMALL TREE TRUNK

LARGE TREE TRUNK

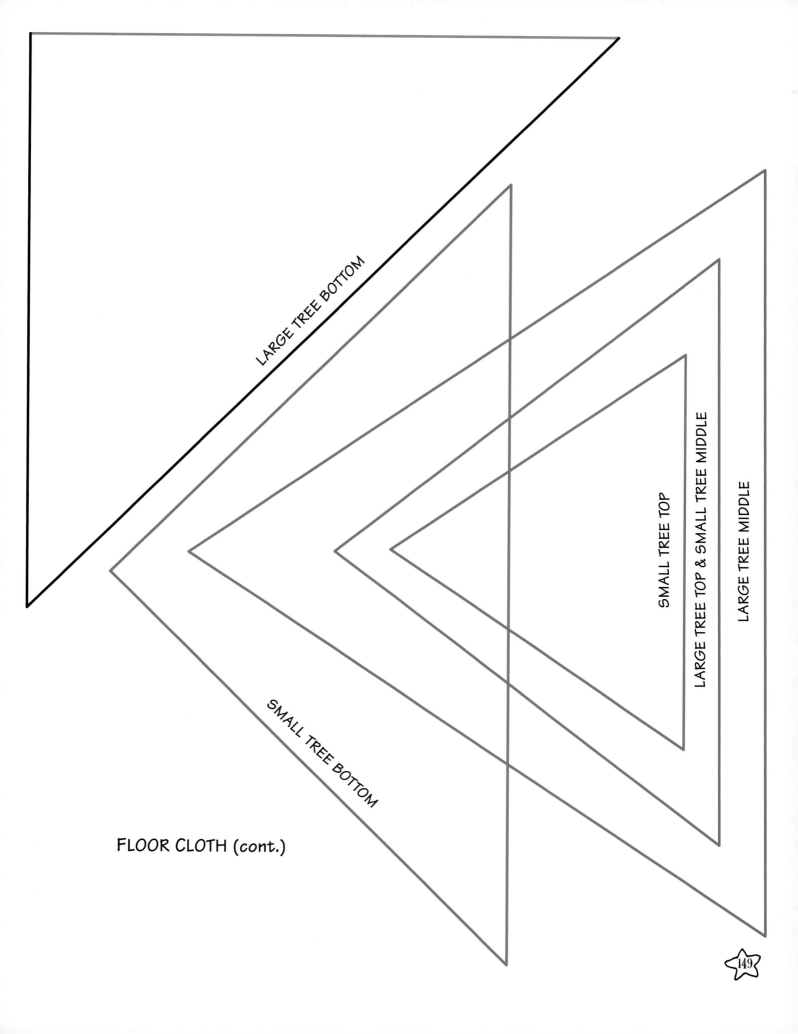

LARGE TREE BOTTOM

SMALL TREE TOP

LARGE TREE TOP & SMALL TREE MIDDLE

LARGE TREE MIDDLE

SMALL TREE BOTTOM

FLOOR CLOTH (cont.)

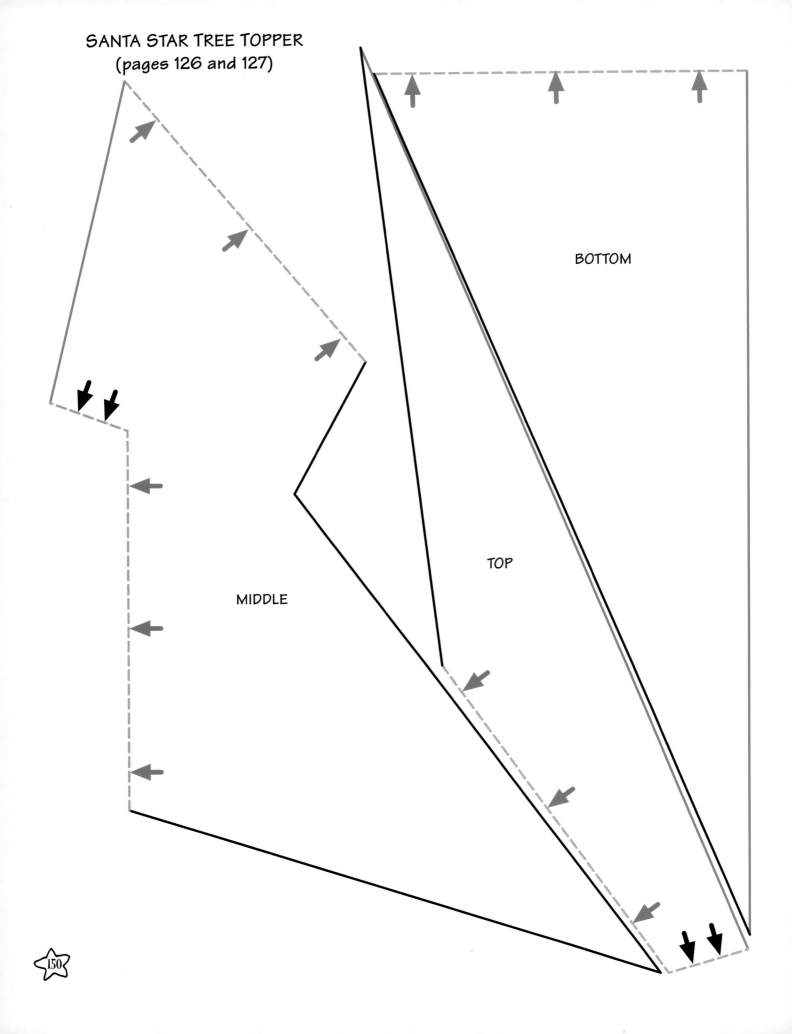

SANTA STAR TREE TOPPER
(pages 126 and 127)

BOTTOM

TOP

MIDDLE

150

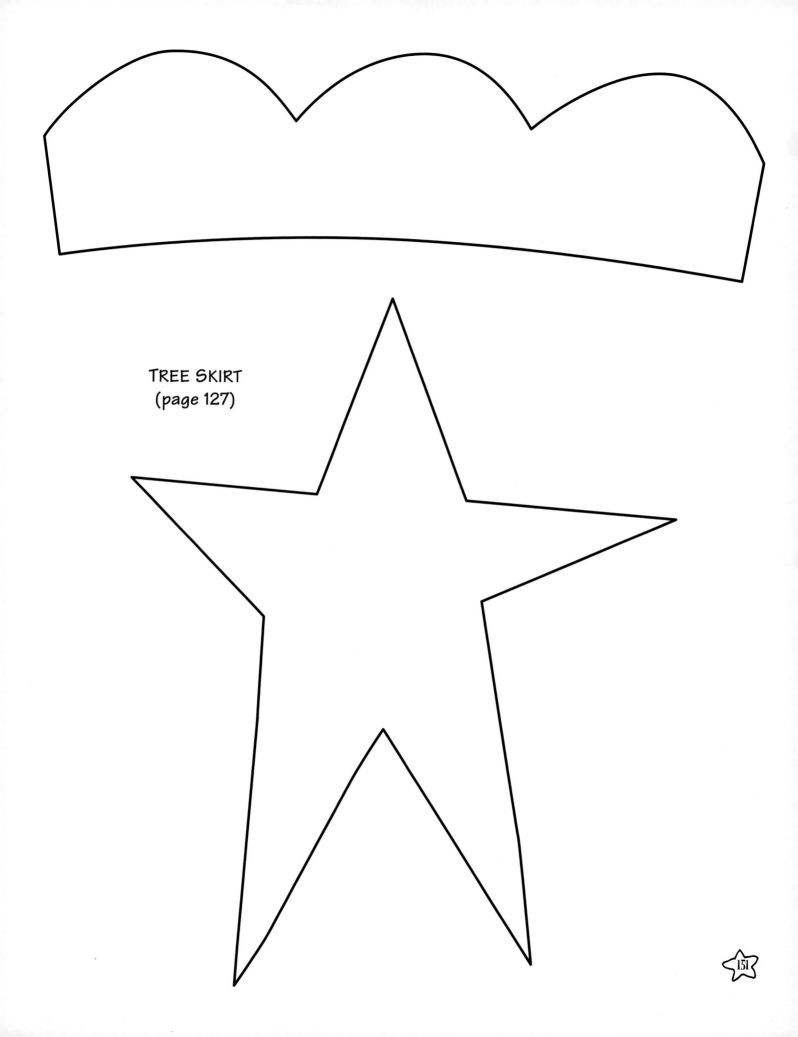

TREE SKIRT
(page 127)

151

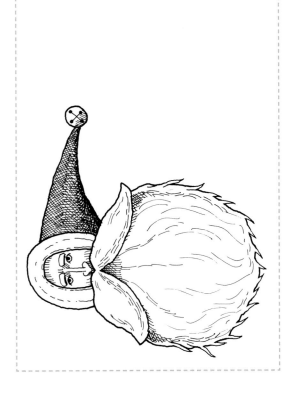

Happy Holidays

PIE TAG
(page 133)

CHRISTMAS BOOKMARKS (page 133)

the best things in life are free.

-OLD SAYING-

Peace on Earth, Good will toward men.

WORDS TO REMEMBER, ESPECIALLY AT CHRISTMAS-TIME:

That best portion of a good man's Life, his Little, nameless, UNREMEMBERED ACTS of KINDNESS and of Love.

– WILLIAM WORDSWORTH –

HOMESPUN GIFT BAG
(page 132)

DATED ORNAMENT
(page 121)

Gooseberry Patch and Leisure Arts, Inc., grant permission to the owner of this book to photocopy the designs on pages 154 and 155 for personal use only.

YULETIDE JARS
(pages 130 and 131)

Happy Holidays

FENCE POST SANTA JAR
(page 132)

SANTA JAR
(page 131)

CARDINAL MITTENS
(page 129)

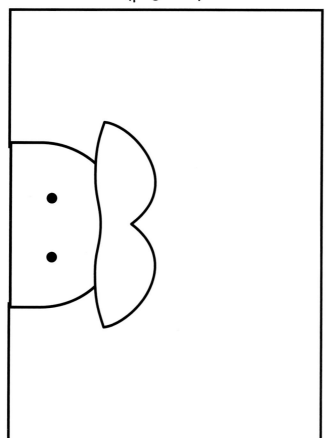

MUG MAT
(page 78)

BREAD CLOTH
(page 132)

A

B

Sweet Noel

A

these shapes Foretell

PROJECT INDEX

RECIPE INDEX

BREADS

CAKES & CHEESECAKES

CANDIES & CONFECTIONS

CONDIMENTS

COOKIES, BARS & BROWNIES

DESSERTS & DESSERT TOPPINGS

DRY MIXES

MAIN COURSES

PIES & PASTRIES

SALADS

SIDE DISHES

SOUPS

Credits

We want to extend a warm *thank you* to the people who allowed us to photograph our projects at their homes: Joan Adams, Carl and Monte Brunck, Charles and Peg Mills and Duncan and Nancy Porter.

We want to especially thank photographers Mark Mathews, Larry Pennington, Karen Shirey and Ken West of Peerless Photography and Jerry R. Davis of Jerry Davis Photography, all of Little Rock, Arkansas, for their time, patience and excellent work.

To Wisconsin Technicolor LLC, of Pewaukee, Wisconsin, we say *thank you* for the superb color reproduction and excellent pre-press preparation.

To the talented designers who helped create the following projects in this book, we extend a special word of thanks:
- Wilma Gilbert: *Primitive Stockings*, 35; *Santa Star Tree Topper*, 52
- Marion Graham: *Family Toboggans*, 68
- Holly R. Witt: *Family Memory Album*, 8-9; *"Dear Santa" Cookie Plate*, 15; *Snowman Pillow*, 26; *Felt Ornaments*, 36-37; *Framed Angel*, 44; *Primitive Angel Ornaments*, 45; *Mitten Garland*, 46-47; *Button Basket*, 63; *Tart Pan Pincushion*, 63; *Fence Post Santa Jar*, 75; *Santa Jar*, 75; *Fabric Bags*, 81
- Kay Meadors: *Christmas Tree Coverlet*, 61

Thanks also go to Kitty Jo Pietzuch, who assisted in making some of the projects in this book.

All's well that ends well. ~old adage

Dear Friend,

During the snowy days of December, hearts and homes are warmed with the simple pleasures of the season...the warmth of a crackling fire, tempting aromas from the kitchen, fragrant baskets of greenery, handmade stockings hanging from the mantel and the glow of candlelight.

*In **Gooseberry Patch Christmas** we've gathered together tasty recipes like Pork Crown Roast, Farmhouse Honey Wheat Bread, Crunchy Granny Smith Salad, Chocolate Snowball Truffles, Gingerbread Coffee Cake and Old-Fashioned Egg Nog. You'll also find quick kitchen mixes for Pancakes & Waffles, Vanilla Coffee and Herbal Spiced Cider...terrific for gift-giving! Handmade gifts are always welcome so we've included lots of ideas with easy-to-follow instructions.*

So before family and friends arrive for long-awaited visits, curl up in a cozy chair, enjoy a cup of cocoa and take time to plan for special homecomings; together you can share all the pleasures of a country Christmas.

Warm Holiday Wishes!
Vickie & JoAnn

ISBN# 1-57486-167-0

90000

9 781574 861679

www.leisurearts.com

108432   U.S. $19.95

7 49075 08432 3

MADE IN U.S.A.